高职高专英语专业系列教材

总主编　常红梅

新世纪英语语法教程

主　编：卢玲蓉
副主编：高新宁　李　防　冯江鸿
编委员：(以姓氏笔画为序)
　　　　卢玲蓉　闫　晗　冯江鸿　杨红全
　　　　李　防　袁　媛　高新宁

图书在版编目（CIP）数据

新世纪英语语法教程 /卢玲蓉主编. —北京：北京大学出版社，2010.4
（高职高专英语专业系列教材）
ISBN 978-7-301-10036-3

Ⅰ. 新⋯　Ⅱ. 卢⋯　Ⅲ. 英语—语法教学—高等学校：技术学校—教材　Ⅳ. H 319.4.

书　　　名：	新世纪英语语法教程
著作责任者：	卢玲蓉　主编
责 任 编 辑：	孙　莹
标 准 书 号：	ISBN 978-7-301-10036-3/H·2281
出 版 发 行：	北京大学出版社
地　　　址：	北京市海淀区成府路205号　100871
网　　　址：	http://www.pup.cn
电　　　话：	邮购部 62752015　发行部 62750672　编辑部 62759634　出版部 62756370
电 子 邮 箱：	zbing@pup.pku.edu.cn
印　刷　者：	北京宏伟双华印刷有限公司
经　销　者：	新华书店
	787毫米×1092毫米　16开本　13.5印张　345千字
	2010年4月第1版　2023年8月第7次印刷
定　　　价：	48.00元

未经许可，不得以任何方式复制或抄袭本书之部分或全部内容。
版权所有，侵权必究　举报电话：010-62752024
电子邮箱：fd@pup.pku.edu.cn

丛书编写说明

　　高等职业教育是我国高等教育体系的重要组成部分,为满足我国社会发展和经济建设需要,促进高等职业教育持续健康发展,教育部积极推进高等职业教育改革,颁布了《高职高专教育英语课程教学基本要求》。北京经济管理职业学院外语系近年来在外语教学上进行了一系列的改革和创新,贯彻先进的教育教学理念,按照岗位要求设置课程、整合教学内容,建立了《实用英语写作》、《商务英语翻译》两门北京市级精品课程,以及《实用英语语法》院级精品课程,《英语阅读》课程也在积极建设之中。高职高专英语专业系列教材正是几年来根据高职教育培养目标的要求,在实践中进行教学内容和课程体系改革的成果。

　　本套教材力图体现我国高职高专英语专业教学实践的特点,遵循高职高专教育"实用为主"、"够用为度"的总体指导方针;教材的设计充分考虑高职高专英语专业的课程设置、课时、教学要求与高职高专英语专业人才培养的要求与目标,强调英语语言基本技能训练与培养实际英语语言能力并重;充分体现了基础性、实用性、够用性和科学性。基础性是指注重语言基础知识,巩固并拓展学生中学阶段的英语知识和能力;实用性是指教材紧扣高职学生的职业方向;够用性是指教材尽可能控制难度,学一点、会一点、用一点,确保学生接受语言信息输入的效果。科学性是指该教材吸收先进的教学理念和方法,符合语言学习规律,恰当、充分地利用现代教育技术手段,有利于教师使用,有利于学生学习。为方便自学,书后提供了练习参考答案。全套四本教材在遵循总的编写原则的同时,又根据各自课程的特点自成体系。

　　高职高专英语专业系列教材包括《新世纪英语写作教程》、《新世纪英语翻译教程》、《新世纪英语阅读教程》和《新世纪英语语法教程》共四本。北京经济管理职业学院的常红梅教授担任总主编,并担任《新世纪英语写作教程》的主编,《新世纪英语语法教程》由卢玲蓉(北京经济管理职业学院)主编,《新世纪英语翻译教程》由孙海红(广东女子职业技术学院)主编,《新世纪英语阅读教程》由薛冰(北京服装学院)主编。

　　高职高专英语专业系列教材涵盖了英语专业及相关专业的骨干课程,旨在构建以核心职业能力培养为主线的理论与实践相结合的特色鲜明的课程教材体系。该系列教材的编写内容是完全根据高职生特点以及职业岗位需求选取,既考虑了高职学生英语基础薄弱,又贯彻了《高职高专英语课程基本要求》对该课程的具体要求,同时又体现了高等职业教育的特色,不仅非常适合高职高专的学生学习,也供普通高校学生、成人学生以及同等英语水平的学生学习和参考。

高职高专英语专业系列教材是身处教学改革第一线的教师们,在深入研究高职教育思想,广泛汲取国内外优秀教材精华的基础上,以创新的意识和大胆改革、勇于实践的精神,经过集体研讨、反复实验而编写完成的。我们期待着这一成果能为推动高职教学改革做出贡献。

编写组

2009年3月

前　言

　　《新世纪英语语法教程》根据《高职高专英语课程基本要求》中对英语语法能力的要求进行编写，以英语教学改革为前提，以高职高专人才培养特点为依据，以培养学生实际运用语言能力为目标，突出教学内容的实用性和针对性，力求做到让学生"学一点、会一点、用一点"。

　　本教材遵循"以学生为主体，以教师为主导"的教学思想，通过图片、问题、例句等方式引导学生思考相关语法现象，以提问的方式引导学生观察例句，发现规律，并通过图示、图表等方式总结、讲解相关语法规则，形式生动活泼，内容简明易懂。每个单元都分为四个部分，即导入、讲解、重点及难点和应用。导入部分通过各种形式和方法，引导学生思考该单元要讲述的语法现象。讲解部分先给出大量例句，让学生观察、思考，然后再用简明的语言解释相应的语法规律。通过思考—观察—思考—总结这样一个过程，让学生能更主动，从而更好地了解语法知识，以避免死记语法规则而不会实际应用到句子中的情况。重点与难点部分主要针对高职学生常遇到的语法问题和困难，并结合高等学校英语应用能力考试的考点，进行进一步补充说明和讲解。应用部分则是相应的练习，旨在巩固所学的语法知识，以期融会贯通，并应用于实际语言中。除了每单元的练习外，我们还把高等学校英语应用能力考试历年真题中语法部分的试题加以分类，并附在相应的章节后，以供备考。

　　从学生的实际需要出发，本教材还编写了四个附录。附录一是自然拼读法。掌握自然拼读法能帮助学生建立英文字母和语音的对应关系，从而有助于学生克服看着单词不敢读，或者大部分单词读不正确的困难。此外，自然拼读法还能在单词记忆和单词拼写方面对学生大有裨益。附录二和三是针对学生词性转换这一薄弱环节设计的词的派生法和常见词和常考词的词性变化表。附录四是学生经常出错的常见动词不规则变化表。

　　全书由北京经济管理职业学院编写。由总主编常红梅进行总体指导；卢玲蓉担任主编，负责统稿，审定修改全文，并负责编写了 Unit 12—16，及附录一；副主编高新宁负责编写了 Unit 1—6，副主编李防负责编写了 Unit 7—9，Unit 17—21，及附录二、三、四，副主编冯江鸿负责编写了 Unit 10—11，闫晗、杨红全、袁媛参与了全书的编写，在此一并表示感谢。

　　需要说明的是本教材在编写过程中，参考了较多的相关著作和教材，并借鉴了一些著作的观点，在此，谨向有关作者表示真诚的感谢。

　　由于编者水平有限，疏漏在所难免，恳请外语界同仁不吝赐教。

卢玲蓉
2009 年 3 月

目 录

Unit 1　简单句 (Simple Sentences) ·· 1
- 简单句概述　● 简单句的五种基本类型　● 并列主语或并列谓语　● 长简单句

Unit 2　并列句 (Compound Sentences) ·· 9
- 并列句概述　● 并列连词　● ... and + too / so / either/ neither 的用法
- Neither..., nor...; Not only... but (also)...; Either... or...

Unit 3　名词从句 (Noun Clauses) ··· 15
- 名词性从句概述　● 主语从句　● 表语从句　● 宾语从句　● 同位语从句
- 从句中的虚拟语气　● 从句的语序　● whether, if 引导的名词从句

Unit 4　定语从句 (Attributive Clauses) ·· 27
- 定语从句概述　● 引导词的选择　● 限定性定语从句和非限定性定语从句
- 定语从句中的介词和关系代词的位置关系　● as 引导的定语从句
- 定语从句和同位语从句的区别

Unit 5　状语从句 (Adverbial Clauses) ··· 37
- 状语从句概述　● 时间状语从句　● 地点状语从句　● 原因状语从句
- 条件状语从句　● 方式状语从句　● 结果状语从句　● 让步状语从句
- 目的状语从句　● 时间状语从句和条件状语从句中不允许使用将来时态
- until 和 till　● 三个表示"一……就……"的固定搭配　● 状语从句中的虚拟语气

真题　从句 ··· 51

Unit 6　There be 句型 ("There be" Sentence Pattern) ························· 55
- There be 句型概述　● There be 句型的语法规则　● Be 动词的一些特殊形式

- There be 句型和情态动词搭配 - There be 句型的非谓语形式 - 其他

Unit 7　强调句 (Emphatic Sentences) ·········· 65
- It is/ was ... that/ who 强调句 - 反身代词强调 - 助动词强调
- not until 结构强调 - 完全倒装表强调 - 部分倒装表强调
- 强调句中 that 的省略

Unit 8　词类和句子成分 (Word Class and Elements of Sentences) ·········· 72
- 词类 - 句子成分 - 表语 - 宾补和双宾语的区别

Unit 9　名词的数和主谓一致 (Number System of Nouns and Subject-verb Concord) ·········· 81
- 可数名词 - 不可数名词 - 主谓一致 - 特殊名词 - 谓语动词用单数的情况
- 谓语动词用复数的情况

Unit 10　动词的种类 (Kinds of Verbs) ·········· 90
- 行为动词 - 系动词 - 助动词 - 情态动词 - 动词短语

Unit 11　动词的时态 (Tenses) ·········· 95
- 一般时态 - 进行时态 - 完成时 - 完成进行时 - 非延续性动词
- 一般现在时和现在进行时表示将来

Unit 12　动词的语态 (Voice) ·········· 103
- 被动语态的基本结构和时态 - 被动语态的适用情况 - 被动语态的特殊结构
- 非谓语动词的被动语态 - 主动语态与被动语态的互换 - 主动形式表示被动

Unit 13　虚拟语气 (Subjunctive Mood) ·········· 110
- 非真实条件句 - 其他从句中的虚拟语气 - 时间错综的非真实条件句
- 非真实条件句的倒装 - 非真实条件句的其他表现形式

真题　时态、语态及虚拟语气 ·········· 118

Unit 14　分词 (Participles) ·········· 122
- 分词的功能 - 分词的其他形式 - 现在分词和过去分词的区别
- 分词的逻辑主语

Unit 15　不定式 (Infinitives) ·········· 128
- 不定式的功能　● 不定式的其他形式　● 不定式与形式主语和形式宾语-it
- 不定式省略 to　● 特殊疑问代词或副词 + 不定式
- 介词 but, except, besides + 不定式

Unit 16　动名词 (Gerunds) ·········· 136
- 动名词的功能　● 动名词的其他形式　● 动名词与不定式　● 动名词的逻辑主语

真题　分词、不定式和动名词 ·········· 143

Unit 17　冠词 (Articles) ·········· 148
- 不定冠词的用法　● 定冠词 the 的用法　● 零冠词

Unit 18　介词 (Prepositions) ·········· 152
- 介词短语的功能　● 介词短语的构成　● 介词辨析

Unit 19　形容词和副词的基本用法 (Basics of Adjectives and Adverbs) ·········· 160
- 形容词的用法　● 副词的用法　● 以 -ly 结尾的形容词
- 多个形容词修饰名词的顺序　● 形容词与副词辨析

Unit 20　形容词和副词的原级、比较级和最高级比较 (Comparison of Adjectives and Adverbs) ·········· 166
- 原级比较　● 比较级比较　● 最高级比较　● 以 -ior 结尾的形容词的用法
- 比较级的特殊用法　● than 前后比较对象的一致性

Unit 21　不定代词 (Indefinite Pronouns) ·········· 171
- one 和 ones 的用法　● each 和 every 的用法　● one, no one 和 none 的用法
- other, others, the other, the others 和 another 的用法　● some 和 any 的用法
- it, one 和 that 的用法

真题　其他类型 ·········· 177

附录一　自然拼读法 (Phonics) ·········· 183

附录二　词的派生法 (Derivation) ·········· 187

附录三　常见词的词性转换 (Conversion of Parts of Speech) ················ **190**

附录四　常见不规则动词变化 (Irregular Verbs) ································ **192**

参考答案 (Answer Key for Reference) ··· **196**

参考文献 (References) ··· **204**

Unit 1　简单句 (Simple Sentences)

我们学会了英文字母就会拼写英文单词,而我们掌握了英文句法就能够读懂并且能够编写英文句子——单词的组合。句子就是包含主语部分和谓语部分的一组词,它有一定的语法结构和语调,能表达一个比较完整的独立概念。(《薄冰通用英语语法》)读懂句子是我们要明白别人说了什么,而编写句子是要别人明白我们说了什么,从而最终达到用英文进行交流的目的。那么什么是句法呢? 句法是 the way words are arranged to form sentences or phrases, or the rules of grammar which control this(单词构成词组或造句的方法,或者是用来控制这一做法的语法规则) (***Longman Dictionary of Contemporary English***);是 grammatical arrangement of words, showing their connection and relation(按照语法规则安排单词,使其能够体现他们之间的关联)(***The Concise Oxford Dictionary***)。可见,句法是一种准则,是我们学、说、写英文必须遵循的一种准则。有了这种准则,我们才能明白彼此的想法和意见,并达到用英文进行准确交流的目的。英语句子分为简单句、并列句、复合句。在这一单元我们先介绍所有句子的基础——简单句。

 导入 (Lead-in)

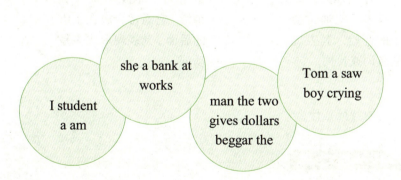

TASK:
用每个圆环中的单词分别组合成一个句子。看看分别是谁做了什么事情或发生了什么状况?

讲解 (Explanation)

● 简单句概述

上面的四个句子分别告诉我们有四个人所做的事或是所处的状态：

1. I am a student.
   我是一个学生。
2. She works at a bank.
   她在银行工作。
3. The man gives the beggar two dollars.
   那个男人给了那个乞丐两块钱。
4. Tom saw a boy crying.
   汤姆看见一个男孩儿在哭。

他们的共同之处就是每个句子中都出现了一个特定的人，并对他进行了描述。也就是每个句子中只有一个主语和一个谓语。

> 简单句是一种句子的组成结构由一个独立的分句构成，并且只包含一个主语和一个谓语。

主语(subject) 是一个句子的主题，它告诉我们在这个句子中是什么样的人或物做了某件事。它通常会放在句子的开始。其表现形式多是名词或代词。

谓语(predicate) 是对主语的描述。它告诉我们在这个句子中发生了什么事情。它通常会放在主语的后面。其表现形式多是动词。

☞ 思考：简单句的特征是什么？

● 简单句的五种基本类型

简单句有下面五种基本的句型结构，其他的各种句子基本上均可以由这五种句型转换而来。

☞ 思考：导入部分中，第一个气球中的句子和其他三个气球中的句子有什么不同呢？
第一个气球中，句子的谓语是由系动词和表语构成的(am a student)；而其他三个气球中，句子的谓语都是实意动词(work, give, see)。

I. 主语+系动词+表语

I'm pretty **busy** these days.
这些天我很忙。
What was that again?
请您再说一遍。/ 您刚才说的是什么？
This is my favorite **song**.
这是我最喜欢听的歌。
I have been here a couple of times.
我已经来过这里两次了。

像上面句子中的 **am, was, is, been** 就是系动词。

> 系动词是一种联系动词，它不能独立使用，其作用就是要联系句子中的两个成分，即主语部分和表语部分。其形式通常表现为 **be**。在肯定句中，放在主语之后表语之前。

而上面句子中的 **busy, that, song, here** 就是表语。

> 表语是对主语的一种补充解释说明，通常的表现形式是形容词或名词。它告诉我们主语的状态或性质，和系动词一起构成句子的谓语部分。

☞ 思考：下面的句子是不是主语+系动词+表语的结构呢？
  1. You look tired today. 你看起来很累。
  2. Your plan seems unworkable. 你的计划看上去无效。
  3. It sounds good. 听起来很好。

这些句子都是主语+系动词+表语的简单句。像 **look, seem, appear, sound, smell, feel, taste** 等感官动词都可以用作系动词。甚至 **go, turn, become** 等一些表示状态上有所变化的动词也可以用作系动词，在后面接形容词作表语。比如：
This kind of food **goes** bad easily.
这类食物容易变坏。
The leaves **turn** yellow in autumn.
树叶到秋天会变黄。
It **became** cold.
天变冷了。

☞ 思考：第二个气球中的句子和第三个气球中的句子有什么不同？

第二个气球的句子中的动词(work)后没有宾语。而第三个气球的句子中的动词(give)后有宾语。

> 宾语(objects)是句子中动作的承受者。它告诉我们在这个句子中,某个动作发生或作用在什么人或物身上。它通常会放在谓语动词后面。其表现形式多是名词或代词。

II. 主语+谓语

My computer *broke*.
我的电脑坏了。
I *am going to leave*.
我要走了。
The girl *is swimming*.
那个女孩正在游泳。
The man over there *is reading*.
那边的那个男的正在看书。

这里的谓语都是实意动词,有明确具体的实际意义,可以独立用作谓语。这些动词是不及物动词。

> 不及物动词(*vi.*)本身具有独立的意思,不需要后面接宾语。如上面句中的 **break, leave, swim** 和 **read**。

※注:我们也可以在句子中加上状语。

> 状语(adverbial modifiers)在句子中描述谓语动词的状态。它告诉我们这个动作发生的地点、时间、环境、方式、原因、程度。其表现形式多是副词或介词短语。它既可以放在谓语前,也可以放在谓语后。

I work **hard**.
我努力地工作。
He **gently** patted me.
她轻轻地拍了拍我。

She **seldom** speaks to other men.
她很少和其他男人说话。
With her help, I passed the exam.
在她的帮助下,我通过了这次考试。

III. 主语+谓语+宾语

I *saved* my work.
我保住了我的工作。
I *want* a sandwich.
我想要一个三明治。
They *are watching* a movie.
他们正在看电影。
The man over there *is reading* a novel.
那边的那个男的正在读小说。

这里的谓语动词都是及物动词。

> 及物动词(vt.)本身不具备独立的意思,它必须要后接宾语才能构成完整的意义。如上面句中的 **save**, **want**, **watch** 和 **read**。

※注:一个动词可以同时具有及物动词和不及物动词的词性。这就表示它既可以接宾语用,也可以不接宾语独立使用。如上面例句中的 **break** 和 **read**。

1. { The cup has **broken**. (*vi.*)　　茶杯碎了。
   { I **broke** the cup. (*vt.*)　　我打碎了茶杯。

2. { She is **reading**. (*vi.*)　　她在读书。
   { She is **reading** a novel. (*vt.*)　　她正在读一本小说。

☞思考:第三个气球内的句子中,在动词 gave 后的 me 和 two dollars 有什么关系?

IV. 主语+谓语+宾语+宾语

Please hand **me** the **salt**.
请把盐递给我。
I wish **you** a good **life**.
我祝你生活幸福。
The teacher told the **children** a **story**.
老师给学生们讲了一个故事。
The photographer showed **us** some of **his works**.
摄影师向我们展示了他的一些作品。

这种简单句中的两个宾语一个是直接宾语,一个是间接宾语。

直接宾语(direct objects)
在句子中是谓语动词所显示动作的承受者。通常是表示物体的名词或代词作直接宾语。

间接宾语(indirect objects)
在句子中是谓语动词所显示动作指向的人或物。通常是表示人的代词或名词作间接宾语。

这类简单句中,直接宾语和间接宾语缺一不可,他们只有和谓语一起才能构成完整的意义。通常情况下,间接宾语位于直接宾语之前。

※ 注:当直接宾语为代词时,间接宾语应该放在直接宾语之后,同时应添加介词 to 或是 for。

Please hand **it** to **me**.
请把它递给我。
The boy told **it** to a **girl**.
这个男孩把它告诉了一个女孩。
The sectary made **this** for the **boss**.
秘书为老板准备了这个东西。

> 在这种结构中的谓语动词都是可以携带双宾语的及物动词。他们被称为双宾语动词或是与格动词。经常会用到的包括:**give, bring, fetch, lend, teach, write, sing, show, offer, leave, buy, get, keep, hand, pass, read, sell, pay, save, send, take, throw, tell** 等。

☞ 思考:你能否找到更多的这种与格动词?

☞ 思考:第四个气球的句子中 crying 是说明修饰谁的? Tom 还是 a boy?

V. 主语+谓语+宾语+补语

I had my hair **cut** yesterday.
昨天我剪了头发。
The newcomer will make all the desks **clean** every morning.
每天早晨这位新来的都会把所有的桌子擦干净。
We call him **hero**.
我们称他是英雄。

I want him *to do* it.
我想让他来做。

这里的补语对句子中的宾语进行描述和说明，是宾语补足语。通常的表现形式为名词、形容词或分词等。

☞ 思考：你还能找到其他的宾语补足语的形式吗？

重点及难点 (Key points)

● 并列主语或并列谓语

简单句中虽然只能有一个主语和一个谓语，但是它们可以是并列主语或／和并列谓语。
Mary and Jones work in the same company.
玛丽和琼斯在同一家公司上班。
The teacher *picked up* the paper *and handed* it to me.
老师拿起卷子，把它递给我。
The boss and the staff walked into the room *and closed* the door.
老板和员工们走进房间，关上了门。

● 长简单句

简单句并非都是短句，有些简单句很长。
Children in big families **have the chance to compete with each other**, in terms of their manners at home, their study at school, their performance at their place of work, etc.
无论是在家的表现、在学校的学习还是在公司的工作表现，大家庭的孩子都有机会互相竞争。
According to the publicity chief of the provincial tourism bureau, Chen Keqin, on the strength of its distinctive geographic and ethnic features, **Yunnan has** the following **advantages for the development of tourism**.
据云南省旅游局宣传负责人陈克勤说，云南省有自己独特的地理和民族特色，凭借这一点，它在发展旅游业方面有如下的几点优势。

 应用 (Practice)

I. Make simple sentences with the following words. Try to make as many sentences as possible. You can add some proper adjectives or adverbs or conjunctives. (用下列所给词尽可能多地编写简单句。可以适当的添加形容词、副词或是连词。)

yesterday	boy	come	Austria	compare	life
she	famer	pain	suffer from	get	better
are	eventually	consult	doctor	feel	tired
wife	cook	meal	sad	is	

II. Try to finish the following simple sentences, using the proper forms of the words in the brackets. (用所给单词的适当形式完成下列简单句。)

1. The sky _____ blue. (appear)
2. Nearly everyone _____ shy in some ways. (be)
3. Other people _____ concerned about the impression. (be)
4. No one ever _____ over being shy completely. (get)
5. Even entertainers _____ the facts. (admit)
6. Perhaps the best reason to do all these preparations _____ to give people a chance to know more about you. (be)
7. The class _____ shown us some wonders. (have)
8. By the end of this year, I _____ English for ten years. (have studied)
9. Neither the clerks nor the manager _____ the work by Friday. (have finished)
10. Blue light from the sun _____ scattered in every way. (be)

III. Finish the following sentences using proper words. (用合适的词完成下列简单句。)

1. The teacher gave all the students _____.
2. Unfortunately, the boy had his leg _____ just before the match.
3. Only she can tell me _____.
4. He first introduced him _____.
5. I lent _____ to one of my classmates.
6. The software can make working on computers _____.
7. On Sundays on the Continent even the poorest put on their best suits, trying to look _____.
8. His messy room wants _____.
9. The chairman began to speak more _____.
10. _____, the man could not have succeeded.

IV. Now you are in an interview, try to introduce yourself with simple sentences. (假设自己在参加面试,用简单句来介绍一下自己。)

Unit 2　并列句 (Compound Sentences)

 **导入 (Lead-in)**

I have used all the creams on the market.

I get indigestion every day.

The room was dark.

Now I am beginning to get bad headaches and pains in my chest.

I turned on the light.

None of them did any good.

把左面的六个句子变成三个句子。

☞ 思考：你可以有多少种方式把上面六个简单句变成三个句子？

 讲解 (Explanation)

● 并列句概述

1. I have used all the creams on the market, **but** none of them did any good.
   我用过了市场上销售的所有乳霜，但是没有一种起作用。
2. I get indigestion every day **and** now I am beginning to get bad headaches and pains in my chest.
   每天我都消化不好，现在头和胸口也开始疼起来。
3. The room was dark **so** I turned on the light.
   屋里很黑，所以我把灯打开。

这三个用 and、but 和 so 连接起来的句子就是**并列句**。

> 并列句(compound sentence)是由两个或两个以上相互平等的具有独立意义的句子并列而成。

I want to buy a new car, but **I don't have enough money.**
我想买一辆新车,但是钱不够。
The girl didn't go home last night, and **now she can not hand in her paper.**
那个女孩昨晚没有回家,现在不能交作业。
He met some trouble, so **I must give him a hand.**
他遇到了一些麻烦,因此我必须帮他一把。

> 并列句的分句有什么特征?

> 并列句中包含的两个或两个以上的分句都是具有独立意义并且结构完整的句子。而且他们之间是完全平等的,不存在任何依附关系。

☞ 思考:并列句的各个分句是靠什么连接的?

重点及难点 (Key points)

● 并列连词

并列句各个分句之间在结构上是平等并列的,他们之间没有从属关系,主次之分。在一个句子中,他们依靠并列连词进行连接构成一个完整的句子。

> 连词(conjunctions)是连接单词、短语、句子的词,属于虚词,不能在句子中单独作成分。并列连词(coordinating conjunctions)主要连接并列结构,可以表达并列、因果、转折、对比等不同的意义。

在句子中,并列连词之前可以用逗号,也可以不用逗号。如果有两个以上的并列分句,通常只在最后一个分句前面用连词,其他句子之间用逗号隔开。

He is reading **and** she is writing.
他在看书,她在写东西。
He is reading, **and** she is writing.
他在看书,她在写东西。

He is reading, she is writing, **and** I am listening.
他在看书,她在写东西,我在听音乐。

> 常用的并列连词有:**and, but, or, yet, so, for, nor, therefore, hence, however, then, not only... but also..., as well as** 等。

※注:

  并列句的各个分句之间在结构上是平等并列的。但是并不是说任意两个句子放在一起用连词连接后就构成一个并列句。并列句的各个分句之间在逻辑意思上必须有一定的联系。

I like driving, **while** she likes walking. (对比)
我喜欢开车,而她喜欢走路。
It is snowing, **so** he was late. (因果)
正在下雪,因此他迟到了。
He talks **and** I listen. (并列)
他说我听。
They found an idea, **but** it didn't work. (转折)
他们想到了一个主意,但是没有用。

☞ 思考:如果把一个并列句拆写成由各个分句构成的几个简单句,会有什么不同的效果?

>   如果一个并列句的各个分句使用的是同一个谓语动词那么在 **but** 和 **and** 的后面通常不会重复这一动词而是用助动词来代替。助动词与谓语动词使用相同的时态。

I **like** coffee, but my father **doesn't**.
我喜欢喝咖啡,但是我父亲不喜欢。
He **isn't** here, but she **is**.
他不在这儿,但是她在。
I **cried**, and the girl **did** too.
我哭了,那个女孩也哭了。

>   **for** 作并列连词表因果关系使用时,不能放置在并列句的句首而只能放置在两个分句的中间。

For Tom is ill, he is absent today. （×）
Tom is absent today, **for** he is ill. （√）
汤姆今天没有来，因为他生病了。

●...and + too / so / either/ neither 的用法：

> 为何助动词要放置于主语之前？

主语 + 助动词 + <u>too</u> = <u>so</u> + 助动词 + 主语（肯定句）
主语 + 助动词 + <u>not</u> + <u>either</u> = <u>neither</u> + 助动词 + 主语（否定句）

{ I earn money, **and** my husband **does too**.
{ I earn money, **and so does** my husband.
我挣钱养家，我丈夫也是如此。

{ I am not late, **and** Rose **isn't either**.
{ I am not late, **and neither is** Rose.
我没有迟到，罗丝也没有。

{ John didn't get the job, **and** Joe **didn't either**.
{ John didn't get the job, **and neither did** Joe.
约翰没有得到这份工作，乔也没有。

※ 注：这里的 neither 可以换成 nor。

I am not late, **nor is** Rose.
John didn't get the job, **nor did** Joe.

● Neither..., nor...; Not only... but (also)...; Either... or...

这三个结构，前两个在连接两个句子时，要用倒装（部分倒装）；另一方面，当两个或几个分句的谓语动词是相同的时候，后面的分句只用相同时态的助动词来代替。而 either... or... 不用倒装结构。

Neither is he wrong, **nor are you**.
他没有错，你也没错。
Neither has he applied for any job, **nor will he** intend to do that.
他以前没有找工作，今后也不打算去找。

Either he is wrong, **or you are**.
或许他错了,或许你错了。
Either he has told a lie, **or somebody has cheated** him.
或许他撒了一个谎,也或许是别人骗了他。
Not only did Paul speak more correctly, **but also he spoke** more easily.
保罗不仅讲得更正确了,也讲得更轻松了。
Not only was she compelled to stay at home, **but also she was forbidden** to see her friends.
她不仅被逼呆在家,还禁止见朋友。

但是如果 not only ... but also... 不放在句首,就用正常的陈述语序而不用倒装。

Paul **not only spoke** more correctly, **but also spoke** more easily.
She **was not only compelled to** stay at home, **but also forbidden to** see her friends.

I. Find out the compound sentences in the following paragraph.(找出下面一段文字中的并列句。)

    A few days ago, a friend and I were driving from Benton Harbor to Chicago. We didn't experience any delays for the first hour, but near Chicago we ran into some highway construction. The traffic wasn't moving at all. My friend and I sat in the car and waited. We talked about our jobs, our families and the terrible traffic. Slowly, the traffic started to move.

II. Choose proper coordinating conjunctions to connect the two sentences.(用合适的并列连词连接两个句子。)

1. This time tomorrow the result of the election will be issued _____ we will know the right person.
2. She may not be at home this afternoon, _____ I shall go and see her anyway.
3. The mother got her son working at mathematics _____ she herself was watching TV.
4. Mrs. Jones does not like shopping, and _____ does she like gardening.
5. Yesterday is history, tomorrow is a mystery, _____ today is a gift.
6. It is a joke, _____ somehow it all seems to make sense.
7. The city at one time was prosperous, _____ it enjoyed a high-level civilization.
8. You can work extra hours to save up your money, _____ you can just sleep.
9. _____ you look at it, it was a wicked thing to do.
10. My mother can _____ sing _____ write songs herself.

III. **Complete the sentences by using too, so, either, or neither and proper verbs if necessary.**（用 too, so, either, or neither 完成下列句子，如有必要可以添加合适的动词。）

1. You will go to the lecture, I shall _____.
2. Your effort will save plenty of money, and it will make others trust you _____.
3. I don't want to buy any of these books, _____ the other girls.
4. I don't like ice tea, and she _____.
5. With so many obstacles, I decided to quit, and _____ the others.

IV. **Try to translate the following sentences into Chinese.**（把下列句子翻译成汉语。）

1. While he likes tea, his brother prefers coffee.

2. They arrived at Bill's home first and Mark was invited in for a Coke and to watch some television.

3. I found several books on the subject but often these were written in a dry and academic way.

4. I can do better and use my sense of humour and personal experiences to help people from both sides of the Atlantic to communicate more effectively, therefore you must trust me.

5. The success of the revived Olympics moved Greece to declare itself the rightful host of all future Games, but de Coubertin and the International Olympic committee were determined to move the athletic feast around.

Unit 3 名词从句 (Noun Clauses)

我们在 Unit 1 提到英语句子分为简单句、并列句和复合句。这一单元我们着重看一下复合句。复合句(complex sentences)由一个主句和一个或者多个从句组合构成。主句是这个句子的主体,而从句是主句的一个成分。它们之间是从属关系。因此复合句中会有多个主谓结构。

```
                复合句
        (complex sentences)
          /            \
      主句       +      从句
(principal sentences)  (subordinate sentences)
```

一个句子的主体,是一个完整的简单句结构,但是句中的某一个或是某几个句子成份是以**句子**的形式出现。

主句的某个句子成份(主语、表语、宾语、补语、状语或是定语等),有完整的句子结构但是不可以独立成句。因为他需要**关联词**的引导。这个关联词把从句和主句连接在一起。主句必须有从句的帮助才会有完整的意思。

用来连接从句和主句的词,常用的有:
although(虽然), **because**(因为), **if**(是否), **that**(没有实际意义), **what**(什么), **whatever**(无论什么) **when**(什么时候), **where**(哪里), **whether**(是否), **which**(哪个), **who**(谁), **why**(为什么)等。

That is **why I came here**. (从句作表语)
那就是我为什么会来这里的原因。
The boss asked me **when I could finish it**. (从句作宾语)
老板问我什么时候能够完成。
I want to go to a place **where no one can find me**. (从句作定语)
我想去一个没有人能找到我的地方。
He left **because no one loved him**. (从句作原因状语)
他走了,因为没有人爱他。

※注:从句的某个或某几个句子成份也可以再用从句来表示。这样就会使句子变得更复杂。

The population control should be carried out in developed countries *because a baby* that is born in the U.S. *will use 30 times* more *of the world's resources* than a baby who is born in India.
发达国家应该实行人口控制,因为出生在美国的孩子消耗掉的世界资源比出生在印度的孩子要多30倍。

> 从句按其在主句中所起的作用可以分为:
> 名词性从句、形容词从句和副词从句。

导入 (Lead-in)

"On the Internet, nobody knows you're a dog."

找找看,图中两只小狗的那句谈话,其中的宾语是什么?

Unit 3　名词从句

讲解 (Explanation)

● **名词性从句概述**

On the Internet, nobody knows you're a dog. 这句话中的宾语部分应该是"**you're a dog**"。很明显这本身也是一个完整的简单句,但是它在对话中充当了宾语的成份,我们就把"**you're a dog**"叫做这句话的宾语从句。其前边省略了关联词 **that**。宾语从句就是一种名词性从句。

> 名词性从句(**noun clauses**)就是可以当作名词使用的从句。因为名词在句中可以用作主语、表语、宾语和同位语,所以名词性从句中也包括有**主语从句、表语从句、宾语从句和同位语从句**。

☞ 思考:_____ is the book. 想想看这句话的主语部分可以放一个什么样的句子?

● **主语从句**

> 主语从句(**subjective clauses**)是可以用作主语的从句。它通常会用到的关联词除了疑问代词和疑问副词(**which, who, what, when, where, why, how, whether, whatever, whoever, wherever, however, etc.**)之外,还有 **that** 等。位置基本上是位于谓语动词之前。

That he has got a promotion is very important to him.
得到提升这件事对他来说非常重要。
What I want to find is a book.
我想找的是一本书。
Whoever wants to get in must sign up here.
任何人想要进来都必须在这里签到。
What you said moved me.
你说的话打动了我。

※ 注:主语从句如果由 **that**(本身无意义), **whether**(是否)引导,那么这些关联词只是用来连接从句和主句,在从句中不充当任何成份。而如果是其他的关联词的话,他们就要在从句中充当某个句子成份。

That he left made me sad.
(that 在从句中不充当任何成份)
他离开让我很伤心。
Why he left is a secret.
(why 在从句中充当原因状语)
他为什么离开是一个秘密。
Who will come is not said.
(who 在从句中充当主语)
没有说谁会来。
What you wear doesn't fit you.
(what 在从句中充当宾语)
你穿的衣服不适合你。

> 主语从句如果放在句首有时会显得句子很笨重,尤其是当主语从句比较长的时候,所以我们常常会把它放在句子的末尾,而用 **it** 放在句首来做形式主语。

★ (It is + *adj.* + clause)
 It is important **that you should be on time on the first day.**
 第一天你应该守时,这是很重要的。

★ (It is + *n.* + clause)
 It has not been a secret **who will be the new manager.**
 谁是新的经理已经不是一个秘密了。

★ (It is + *n.* + clause)
 It is a fact **that you will go and do it yourself.**
 事实是你要去并且亲自做。

★ (It is + past participle + clause)
 It is said **that we have found a new planet to live on.**
 据说我们已经发现了一个新的可以居住的星球。

★ (It + *vi.* + clause)
 It happened **that we chose the same gift.**
 碰巧我们选了一样的礼物。

☞ 思考:如果上面各句不用形式主语 it,又会怎样?

● 表语从句

> **表语从句**(predicative clauses)是可以用作表语的从句。它通常会用到的关联词除了 **what, who, when, where, which, why, whether, how, etc.** 之外，还有 **that, as if**(好像), **as though**(好像), **because** 等。位于主句的系动词之后。

This is **what I want.**
这就是我想要的。

The fact is **that the girl married another man.**
事实是这个女孩嫁给了另外一个男人。

It looks **as if it is going to snow.**
看起来好像要下雪。

It seems **that you have forgotten what you had said.**
好像你已经忘了你曾说过的话。

That is **because you made a right choice.**
那是因为你做了正确的抉择。

※ 注：表语从句的关联词 **that** 在从句中没有任何实际意义，不充当任何成份，可以省略掉。

The fact is **(that)** the girl married another man.
It seems **(that)** you have forgotten what you had said.

☞ 思考：设想一些情境使我们可以用到表语从句！

● 宾语从句

> **宾语从句**(objective clauses)是可以用作宾语的从句。它通常会用到的关联词除了 **what, who, when, where, which, why, whether, how, etc.** 之外，还有 **that, if** 等。它通常放在谓语动词后面，也可以放在介词、不定式、动名词、分词还有形容词后面作宾语。

I agree **that it is going to snow.**
我同意马上要下雪了。

The teacher asked **why he was late.**
老师问他为什么迟到。

Unit 3　名词从句

I'm sure **where he lives.**
我知道他住哪儿。
I don't know **if she is married.**
我不知道她是否结婚了。
He is not interested in **what we are doing.**
他对我们正在做的事不感兴趣。
Seeing **that the teacher was not in,** they began to talk with each other.
看到老师不在,他们开始互相聊了起来。

※ 注:
① 由 **that** 引导的宾语从句,因为 **that** 没有任何意义且在从句中不充当任何成份,因此经常会被省略掉,尤其是在口语和非正式文体中。

I agree (**that**) it is going to snow.
我也认为马上要下雪了。
I am afraid (**that**) he will not come today.
恐怕他今天不会回来了。
Seeing (**that**) the teacher was not in, they began to talk with each other.

② 在 **think, believe, suppose, expect** 等表示观点、意见、想法的动词所跟的宾语从句中,如果从句是否定形式,通常要把否定词放在主句谓语上,而从句用肯定形式。

{ I think (that) I don't know you. (×)
{ I **don't** think (that) I know you. (√)
　　我认为我不认识你。

{ I suppose (that) he will not come. (×)
{ I **don't** suppose (that) he will come. (√)
　　我觉得他不会来。

③ 如果主句结构是主语＋谓语＋宾语＋补语,也就是说宾语从句后面还有补语,那么我们就要把这个从句放到补语后面,而宾语从句原来的位置要用 it 来代替。这个 it 叫做形式宾语。

We think **it** wrong **that you came without telling him.**
我觉着你不告诉他就来是不对的。
You'd better make **it** sure **whether he will come or not.**
你最好弄清楚他究竟会不会来。

④ 宾语从句的时态要和主句的时态相呼应,但是当宾语从句表示的是客观真理或是

自然现象的时候，其时态不受主句的影响，要永远用一般现在时。

The baby **was told** that his toy **had been lost**.
人们对这个孩子说，他的玩具丢了。

The baby **was told** that the sun **rises** from the East.
这个孩子被告知太阳从东方升起。

⑤ 在对话中，如果用到 **hope, believe, suppose, guess, think, I'm afraid** 等词来回答 yes 或 no 的问题，那么常用 **so** 跟在这些动词后面来代替上句提到的内容。

{ —Is he married?
　—**I think so. / I don't think so.**
　—他结婚了吗？
　—我认为结了。/ 我认为没结。

{ —Will your mother come?
　—**I hope so. / I hope not.**
　★I don't hope so.（×）
　—你妈妈来吗？
　—我希望她来。/ 我希望她不要来。

{ —Is what he said true?
　—**I guess so. / I guess not.**
　—他说的是真的吗？
　—我想是真的。/ 我觉着不是真的。

● 同位语从句

同位语从句（**appositive clauses**）是可以用作同位语的从句。它通常会用到的关联词是 **that**，有时也会用到疑问词形式的引导词。它一般会紧跟在其解释的名词后面，但有时为了句子的结构平衡，也会被其它词隔开。

同位语是句子中跟在某个名词或代词后面的名词或代词。它用来解释说明前者的性质和情况或内容。两者在句中所起的作用是相同的。我们把后者称作前者的同位语。

He told us his decision **that he would quit**.
他告诉我们他决定辞职。

Nobody can answer the question how it was done.
这是如何做到的，没有人能回答这样的问题。

His idea that we do it together is worth considering.
他认为我们应该一起做这个想法值得考虑。

The final decision whether we should accept it or not will be left to the boss.
我们是否接受的最终决定由老板来做。

> 常用的能带同位语从句的名词有：fact, belief, news, idea, truth, decision, suggestion, question, information, order 等，它们都具有某种内容含义。

☞ 思考：为什么只能是具有某种内容含义的名词才能够有同位语从句？

重点及难点 (Key points)

● 从句中的虚拟语气

虚拟语气可以用在从句中以特定的形式表示一种非真实的状态或者某个人的假设，臆想，猜测或是愿望。

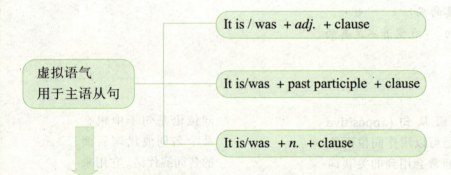

It is important that you (should) follow what I said.
你应该按照我说的做，这一点非常重要。

It is suggested that we (should) have a further discussion.
有人建议说,我们应该更深入地讨论一下。

It is natural that he (should) marry her.
很自然他会娶她。

It was arranged that Mary (should) come back in three days.
按照安排,玛丽应该三天后回来。

※ 注: 这种主语从句的关联词是 that, 常用的形容词和过去分词有:**important, necessary, natural, requested, essential, eager, impossible, possible, probable, recommended, vital, arranged** 等。

虚拟语气
用于宾语从句

- 用在 wish 后面,表示不可能实现的愿望。用过去时态或是过去完成时态。常省去 that

- 用在 would rather 或是 would sooner 后面,表示愿望。用过去时态或是过去完成时态。常省去 that

- 用在 demand, order, propose, request, require, suggest, desire, command, urge, prefer, recommend 等表示建议,命令,要求等的动词后面。用 should + 动词原形 的形式。should 可省略。

I wish I were you. (对现在的愿望)
我希望我是你。
I wish you had done it. (对过去某件事情的愿望)
我希望你已经完成了。
I would rather you came tomorrow than today. (对现在发生事件的愿望)
我宁愿你明天来而不是今天。
I would rather you had told it to me. (对过去发生事件的愿望)
我宁愿你早已经告诉我了。
He suggested that we (should) do it now.
他建议我们现在就做。

The boss ordered that he **(should) go** by train.
老板命令他坐火车去。

> 虚拟语气
> 用于表语从句 ── 从句用 **should**+动词原形 的形式。引导表语从句的关联词常用 **that**，并且可以省略。

> 主句中的主语通常是：suggestion, proposal, idea, order, recommendation, plan, request 等。

The doctor's **suggestion** is (that) he **(should) relax.**
医生建议他休息。

His **plan** is that he **come** back to his hometown after the graduation.
他计划毕业之后回自己的家乡。

● 从句的语序

由于疑问词可以做关联词引导名词性从句，所以当我们使用这类从句时需要注意疑问词后面的从句要使用陈述句的语序，即简单句的五种基本结构之一，而不能使用疑问句的倒装语序。

I know what do you want to do. (×)
I know **what you want to do.** (√)
我知道你想做什么。

Where does the movie star live is a secret. (×)
Where the movie star lives is a secret. (√)
这位影星住在哪里是一个秘密。

● whether, if 引导的名词从句

whether 和 **if** 在引导从句时虽然汉语意思基本相同，但是 **whether** 可以引导主语从句、宾语从句、表语从句和同位语从句，但是 **if** 只能引导宾语从句而且后面不跟 or not.

It made me crazy **if** you will choose me. (×)
It made me crazy **whether** you will choose me or not. (√)
你会不会选我这个问题把我弄疯了。

{ My doubt is **if** he will keep his promise. (×)
  My doubt is **whether** he will keep his promise or not. (√)
  我怀疑他是否会遵守他的诺言。

 应用 (Practice)

I. Make sentences with Noun Clause to express the following meaning.（用带名词性从句的复合句来表述下列的各个意思。）

1. 毫无疑问，这个国家仍存在着贫困问题。

2. 美国人似乎一直不停地搬家。

3. 我们不明白他到底用了什么办法使得那家公司最终同意签约。

4. 恐怕我不能按照你的要求完成这项工作。

5. 也许这就是那些妻子们非常满意的原因吧。

6. 大家都认为新来的那个人不会接受这样的条件。

7. 这个孩子认为父亲不相信自己说的话。

8. 我的计划是三年之内接管这家公司。

II. Change the following simple sentences into complex sentences with Noun Clauses. (把下面的简单句转换成带有名词性从句的复合句。)

1. An elderly gentleman came to ask me for direction to the public library.
2. He needs to contact his assistant right away.
3. The boss has told me the reason for firing me, but I think it ridiculous.
4. I have a plan.
   I am going to take the kids to the amusement park tomorrow morning.
5. You should let the others know something.
   People can trust you.
   This is very important.

III. What do the following sentences mean? (把下列句子翻译成汉语。)

1. It doesn't make much difference whether he attends the meeting or not.

2. It is reported that so far, foreign financial institutions have made their way into nineteen cities in China.

3. The greatest advantage of books does not always come from what we remember of them, but from their suggestions.

4. What we need is a widespread awareness that once you leave you can never come back.

5. Some young women find it very difficult to come to terms with the feeling that characteristics of authority are often not acceptable in women.

IV. **Complete the following sentences in as many ways as possible.**
(以尽可能多的方式完成下列的句子。)
1. It is impossible that _____.
2. It is arranged that _____.
3. I would rather that _____.
4. The principal requested that _____.
5. One of the best suggestions is that _____.

Unit 4　定语从句 (Attributive Clauses)

导入 (Lead-in)

把我介绍给你的朋友吧！你有多少种方式描述我？

This is a(n) _____ dog.

☞ 思考：你会在这里放什么样的形容词？如果让你放一个句子呢？

讲解 (Explanation)

● 定语从句概述

This is a **lovely** dog.
This is a **clever** dog.
This is a **cute** dog.
This is a **brown** dog.

我们可以在空格处填写 lovely, clever, cute, brown 等形容词来修饰限定这只小狗。这些词在句子中充当 dog 的定语。

> 定语(**attributives**)是一个句子中用来修饰限制某个名词的部分。它告诉我们这个名词的形状、状态、特征与品质，我们可以通过它了解这个名词的相关信息。它通常会放在所修饰词的前面，其表现形式多为形容词、名词、代词、分词等。

现在看下面的这两种表述方式：

This is a dog that has big eyes.
这是一只长着大眼睛的狗。

This is a dog that one of my friends gave to me.
这是我一个朋友送给我的小狗。

这里我们不是在 dog 前而是在 dog 后，不是用一个词而是用一个句子来作定语，修饰限定 dog, 这个句子就叫做定语从句。

> 定语从句(**attributive clauses**)是在一个句子中用来作定语的句子。它可以修饰限制代词或是名词，用来描述它们或是提供它们的相关信息。定语从句跟在其所修饰词的后面。这个词叫做<u>先行词</u>，而先行词和定语从句要依靠<u>引导词</u>连接。

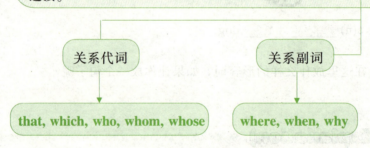

Two boys whom I don't know came in.
我不认识的两个男孩走进来。

The man whose car was stolen called the police.
丢车的男人打电话报警。

The hotel where I lived was clean and comfortable.
我住过的那家酒店既干净又舒适。

引导词除了连接定语从句和先行词之外，还代替先行词在从句中担任一定的语法功能，充当从句中的主语、宾语、定语或是状语。如上面例句中的 that, whom, whose, where 分别作定语从句中的主语、宾语、定语和状语。再如：

I know a <u>man</u> **who is a famous actor**.
我认识一个男人是著名的演员。
I lost the <u>book</u> **which you lent to me**.
我把你借给我的那本书弄丢了。
Tell me the <u>time</u> **when you met each other**.
告诉我你们见面的时间。
You'd better tell us the <u>reason</u> **why you were late**.
你最好告诉我们你迟到的原因。

☞ 思考：如何选择定语从句的引导词？

重点及难点 (Key points)

● 引导词的选择

关系代词可以代替表示人或物的先行词，在定语从句中作主语、宾语或是定语。而关系副词可以代替表示时间、地点或原因的先行词，在定语从句中作时间、地点或是原因状语。

★ **whose** 在从句中作定语，表示先行词与其后面名词的所属关系。……的……。
I'm looking for a <u>book</u> **whose** cover is green.
我正在找一份封皮是绿色的书。
Have you met the <u>girl</u> **whose** scarf is red?
你见过一个围红围巾的女孩吗？

★ **who** 的先行词是表示人的代词或名词，它在从句中作主语。
Have you met the <u>girl</u> **who** is carrying a big black bag?
你见过一个提着大黑包的女孩吗？
We will help those <u>people</u> **who** need it.
我们要帮助那些需要帮助的人。

★ **whom** 的先行词是表示人的代词或名词，它在从句中作宾语。
Have you met the <u>girl</u> **whom** the boss is talking with?
你见过那个正和老板谈话的女孩吗？
The <u>man</u> **whom** you saw yesterday came here today.
你昨天看到的那个男人今天来了。

※ 注：**whom** 通常只用于正式文体中，在口语中以及非正式文体中通常用 **who** 来替代 **whom**。

The man who I called gave me some information.
我打过电话的那个人告诉我一些消息。
I will have a meal with the man who you have introduced to me.
我要和你介绍给我的那个人吃个饭。

★ which 的先行词是表示物的代词或名词，它在从句中既可以作主语也可以作宾语。
The information which I found on the Internet helped me a lot.
我在网上找到的信息帮了我很大的忙。
He gave me some suggestions which were very helpful.
他给了我一些非常有益的建议。

★ that 的先行词是既可以表示物也可以表示人的代词或名词，它在从句中也是既可以作主语也可以作宾语。
The teacher asked the student a question that he can not answer.
老师问了这位学生一个他不能回答的问题。
Where I can catch the bus that goes to the Tiananmen Square?
我在哪里能搭上去天安门广场的汽车？
I want you to know the man that is over there.
我想让你认识站在那边的那个人。
Make friends with those people that you can trust.
要和那些你信任的人交朋友。

※ 注：有些情况下只能用 that 来作引导词。
① 先行词为不定代词时，如：something/somebody, everything/everybody, anything/anybody, nothing/nobody, none, all, few, little, much 等。
Is there anything that you want to buy?
你有什么想要买的东西吗？
I want to tell you something that I have heard.
我想告诉你我刚听到的一些事。
All the people that come today will be hired.
今天来的所有人都会被录取。
I thank you for all that you have given to me.
我为你所给予我的一切而感谢你。

② 先行词由序数词或是形容词的最高级修饰。
It is the most expensive bag that I have ever seen.
这是我所见过的最贵的包了。
You are the second one that can answer the question.
你是第二个能回答这个问题的人。

③ 先行词由 the only, the very, the same, the last 修饰。
He is the very person that I want to talk to.
他正是我想要与之谈谈的人。
You are the only one that can finish the job.
你是唯一一个可以完成这份工作的人。
He is the last person that I will turn to.
我最不愿意向他寻求帮助。

④ 先行词中既有表示人的词，又有表示物的词。
You can choose the people and the device that you prefer.
你可以选择你喜欢的人和设备。
We are talking about the room and the persons that are in our memory.
我们正在谈论我们记忆中的房间和人。

⑤ 主句是 who 或是 which 引导的特殊疑问句时，为了避免重复。
Who wrote this letter that is so beautiful?
谁写了这么美的一封信？
Which one that is on the second shelf will you take?
你要买第二个架子上的哪一个？

★ when 的先行词是表示时间的名词或代词，它在从句中作时间状语。
I will never forget the day when we met for the first time.
我永远也不会忘记我们第一次见面的那一天。
The applicant asked the boss the time when he could come to work.
竞聘者问老板自己什么时候可以来上班。/ 竞聘者问老板自己可以来上班的时间。
This is the right day when he left ten years ago.
今天正是他十年前走的日子。/ 十年前的今天他走了。
It is a time when you can enjoy yourself.
那时候你可以尽情享受美好时光。

★ where 的先行词是表示地点和方位的名词或是代词。他在从句中作地点状语。
The company where he has worked for ten years is going to close.
他工作了十年的这间公司就要倒闭了。
You'd better do your homework in a place where I can see you.
你最好在我能看到你的地方写作业。
This is a country where the people from all over the world gather together.
这是一个来自全世界各地的人们相聚的国度。

★ why 的先行词是表示原因的名词或是代词，在从句中作原因状语。
This is the reason why he didn't show up?
这就是他不来的原因。
I don't know the reason why he married someone who he doesn't love at all.
我不知道他为什么娶了一个他根本不爱的人。
There are several reasons why he quit.
他辞职的原因有很多。

● 限制性定语从句和非限制性定语从句

定语从句可以分为限制性定语从句和非限制性定语从句。

> **限制性定语从句**对主句的内容进行限定性阐释说明，是主句不可或缺的一部分，如果去除，会影响句子的意义。它主要修饰先行词，紧跟在先行词之后，并且从句和主句之间不需要逗号隔开。可以由任一个引导词引导。

> **非限制性定语从句**对主句的内容进行附加性补充说明，如果去除，并不会影响改变主句的意义表达。它既可以修饰先行词也可以修饰整个句子，而且从句和主句之间需要逗号隔开。不可以由 that 引导。

The country **which / that he has just visited** is trying to attract visitors from all over the world.（限制性定语从句）
他刚刚游览的那个国家正努力吸引来自全世界各地的游客。
China, **which is full of enthusiasm,** opens the door to the world.（非限制性定语从句，补充说明 China）
中国——这个充满热情的国度，正向世界敞开她的大门。
Too much stress is harmful to your health, **which is well-known to all.**（非限制性定语从句，修饰说明整个主句。）
众所周知，太多的压力对健康有害。

● 定语从句中的介词和关系代词的位置关系

这里我们所讲的是当 whom, which 和 that 作定语从句中介词的宾语时，它们的位置关系。
The man **whom / that I told you about** is over there.
（whom/that 作 tell... about 的宾语。）
我跟你说过的那个男人现在在那边。

The hotel **which / that we lived in** is clean and comfortable.
（which/that 作 lived in 的宾语。）
我住过的那个旅馆既干净又舒适。
My father is someone **that I can always depend on.**
（that 作 depend on 的宾语。）
我的父亲是一位我永远都可以依靠的人。

在非常正式的英语表达中，定语从句中动词后面的介词会置于定语从句的句首即关系代词的前面，这时只能用 which 或是 whom 而不能用 that。
The man **about whom I told you** is over there.
The hotel **in which we lived** is clean and comfortable.
My father is a person **on whom I can always rely.**

※ 注：

> 当定语从句中的介词放在动词之后时，whom, which 和 that 都可以省略。

The man **I told you about** is over there.
The hotel **we lived in** is clean and comfortable.
My father is someone **I can always depend on**.

> 固定动词词组中的介词不可以前置，只能放在动词后面。

He didn't find the person **whom / that he was looking for.**
他没有找到他刚才在找的人。
I accepted the money **which / that he had taken out.**
我收下了他拿过来的钱。

> 事实上，介词 +which 的结构相当于关系副词的用法。

The hotel **where / in which** I lived is clean and comfortable.
I can not forget the day **when / on which** we graduated from the college.
我不能忘记我们大学毕业的那一天。
Can you tell me the reason **why / for which** he came here.
你能告诉我为什么他会来这儿吗？

as 引导的定语从句

as 引导定语从句一般都是有固定的搭配用法，如：the same... as, such... as, so... as, as we all know, as is known to all, as is said, as already mentioned above, as is usual, as is often the case, as is reported 等，表示"就像……，正如……"的意思。

As is usual, the sectary prepared everything well for the boss this morning.
就像往常一样，秘书今天早晨为老板做好了一切准备。
I have never seen **such** kind of student **as she is.**
我从来没有见过像她那样的学生。
I have **the same** dress **as you wear today.**
我有一件和你今天穿的一样的衣服。
As she said, the beautiful patterns on the dishes gave her pleasure.
正如她所说的，她看到盘子漂漂亮亮的就很高兴。

定语从句和同位语从句的区别

☞ 思考：如何理解下面两句话。that 引导的从句都翻译成 fact 的定语吗？

I know the fact that you have already quit.
I know the fact that you found yesterday.

第一个句子中的 that 从句是同位语从句，它是 fact 的内容，翻译时要体现出来：我知道你早已辞职这一事实。而第二个句子中的 that 从句是定语从句，修饰限定 fact，翻译时要注意：我知道你昨天发现的那个事实。在第一个句子中我们知道这个 fact 是什么内容，而在第二个句子中，我们不知道 fact 的内容，只知道它是"你"发现的。

① 同位语从句是对先行词的具体内容进行说明，他们之间是平等的关系。一般来讲，先行词和同位语从句可以构成一个带有表语从句的主系表结构的复合句。就像上面第一个句子我们可以在 fact 和同位语之间加一个 is，其逻辑关系是成立的：(√)The fact is that you have already quit. 而第二个句子中的 fact 和从句之间是不能加 is 的，其逻辑关系不成立：(×)The fact is that you found yesterday. 这个句子是不成立的。

② 同位语从句可以由 whether, what, how 来引导，而定语从句不可以由这三个词来引导。(详见"同位语从句"和"定语从句"的解释。)

③ 同位语从句中的引导词 that 在从句中不作任何成份，没有任何意义，只起到连接的作用。而定语从中的引导词 that 在从句中可以充当主语或是宾语并且要代替先行词有一定

的意义。像上面需要思考的两个句子,第一个句子中的 that 没有实际意义,可以省略。而第二个句子中的 that 要代替 fact 作 found 的宾语。正因为这样,同位语从句没有引导词也是一个完整的句子结构,而定语从句若没有引导词却是不完整的句子,它需要引导词来作主语或是宾语。

 应用 (Practice)

I. **Use proper attributive clauses to make the following simple sentences more complete and richer.**(用合适的定语从句改写下面的简单句。)
　1. I am talking with a woman.
　2. I have some good friends.
　3. I want to find a job.
　4. Camel is a kind of animal in the desert.
　5. The girl managed to be enrolled by a famous university.

II. **Translate the following sentences.**(中英文互译)
　1. The tree branch which was lying in the street was a hazard to motorists.
　2. Pizza that is sold by piece is a popular lunch in many cities and towns throughout the world.
　3. The woman who was sitting in front of me at the movie was wearing a big hat.
　4. The bank from which I borrowed money charges high interest on its loans.
　5. Television, it is often said, keeps one informed about current events, allows one to follow the latest developments in science and politics, and offers an endless series of programs which are both instructive and entertaining.
　6. 百货店主就是拥有或经营商店的人。
　7. 像平常一样,老板一进门就把包和大衣扔到秘书的桌子上。
　8. 他把那份文件丢了,这使得我们前一阵的工作都白做了。

III. Try to use some proper sentences with attributive clauses to describe what you see.（用带有定语从句的复合句描述你在图片中所看到的内容。）

IV. Make a dialogue with adjective clauses.（用有定语从句的句子编写一段对话。）

V. Change the two or more sentences into one with attributive clauses.（把下面每个练习中的两到三句话用定语从句连接成一个句子。）

1. Many of the problems have existed since the beginning of recorded history.
   Many problems exist today.
2. A man is standing over there.
   I want to introduce you to that man.
3. Monkeys will eat almost anything.
   They can find a lot of things.
4. I read a magazine at the doctor's office.
   The magazine had an interesting article.
   You ought to read the article.
5. It is important for all children to have at least one adult.
   The children can form a loving, trusting relationship with the adult.

Unit 5　状语从句 (Adverbial Clauses)

导入 (Lead-in)

I saw a girl.
I walked out.

We are good friends.
I will not tell you that.

I was late.
I was asked to see the boss.

TASK:
把上面的三组句子连成三个句子，有多少种组合方式？

讲解 (Explanation)

在你写出的句子中有没有这样的呢？
When I walked out, I saw a girl.
I was asked to see the boss **because I was late.**
Although we are good friends, I will not tell you that.

在这里连接每两个句子的词（when, because, although）是从属连词，而跟在从属连词后面的句子叫作状语从句。

● 状语从句概述

The seeds will take root **wherever there is water**.
有水的地方种子就能发芽。

I will do it **if you provide enough power.**
如果你给我足够的权力，我来做。
I left my doggie at home **because the pet is not allowed.**
我把我的小狗留在家里因为不允许带宠物。

> 状语从句(adverbial clauses)是在一个复合句中用来作状语的句子。它修饰和描述主句中的动词或是形容词，给我们提供和它们相关的 when, where, why, to what degree 或 under what conditions 这类的信息。状语从句跟在从属连词的后面，位于主句的前面或是后面。

> 从属连词 (subordinate conjunctions)是用来连接状语从句和主句的连词。它一般是状语从句的标志。我们常用的从属连词有：after, before, unless, although, if, until, as, in order that, when, as if, since, whenever, as long as, so that, where, as soon as, than, wherever, because, though, while 等。

状语从句的位置不是很固定，它既可以放在主句之前也可以放在主句之后，但是如果把它放在句首的话，那么从句和主句之间要用逗号隔开。状语从句一般分为：**时间状语从句、地点状语从句、原因状语从句、条件状语从句、方式状语从句、结果状语从句、让步状语从句和目的状语从句。**

☞ 思考：不同的状语从句提供给我们的分别是有关主句动词或形容词的什么信息呢？

● 时间状语从句

When I walked out, I saw a girl.
我出来的时候看到了一个女孩。
I think I can finish the work **before you get here.**
我想我能在你来之前把工作做完。
I have been here for twenty years **since I married him.**
自从嫁给他，我在这里已经有二十年了。
The father will **not** come back **until he earns enough money.**
这位父亲挣了足够的钱之后就会回来。

时间状语从句告诉我们主句动词所表示动作发生的时间。它描述的是主句动词发生时间和从句动词发生时间之间的关系。即之前、之后、或是同时等。

I was talking with someone on the phone when the door bell rang.
当门铃响的时候我正在和一个人讲电话。

After you have found the evidence, you can come for me.
你找到证据之后，就可以来找我。

> 常用的连接时间状语从句的从属连词有：when, before, after, as（当……时，一边……一边），while, since, whenever, once, until, till, as soon as 等。

※ 注：while 更强调主句和从句中的两个动作同时发生，它不可以表示一个时间点。as 也是一样。

While I finish my homework, I will go with you. (×)
When I finish my homework, I will go with you. (√)
等我写完作业就和你去。
While I was doing my homework, he came in. (√)
我正在写作业他进来了。

● 地点状语从句

He works where his mother was born.
他在他妈妈出生的地方工作。
Where there is a will, there is a way.
有志者事竟成。
Finally, he decided to go where his father expects him to.
最终，他还是决定去父亲希望他去的地方。

地点状语从句告诉我们主句动词所表示动作发生的地点。它描述的是主句动词所表示动作和从句动词所表示动作发生地点的位置关系。

I will go wherever you go.
你去哪儿我就去哪儿。
Most of us would rather spend our time where we can find some fun.
我们大多数人宁愿在我们能找到乐趣的地方打发时间。

> 常用的连接地点状语从句的从属连词有：where, wherever 等。

☞ 思考：用 where 引导的定语从句和地点状语从句有何区别？

● 原因状语从句

I was asked to see the boss **because I was late**.
我迟到了,因此被老板叫去。
The biggest headache is our dormitory **because we need the electric light even in day**.
最让我们感到头疼的是宿舍,因为即使是在白天也需要开灯。
I love my job **because it can make the public place more beautiful**.
我热爱我的工作,因为它能让公众场所更加漂亮。
Because I don't care how much money I earn, I am still here.
因为我不在乎挣多少钱,所以我现在仍在这儿。

原因状语从句告诉我们主句动词所表示动作发生的原因。它描述主句动词所表示动作或状态和从句动词所表示动作或状态之间的因果关系:因为有了后者的发生才有前者的出现。一般翻译成"由于……、因为……、……因此……"等。

Since you have told me the secret, I will show you the truth.
既然你已经告诉我这个秘密,我就告诉你事实真相吧。
As she has quit, you will supervise this team.
由于她已经辞职,那么由你来负责这个团队。
My life is fulfilling because I get tremendous satisfaction from my friends.
我的生活很充实因为我从朋友们那里得到太多的满足。

> 常用的连接原因状语从句的从属连词有:**because, since, as, now that, considering** 等。

※ 注:这些从属连词中,**because** 表达的因果关系最强势,语气最重。在回答 **why** 的提问时,必须用 **because**。

She didn't complete the project **because it is hard for her**.
因为这个项目对她来说太难了,所以他没有完成。
Since it is your first time, you can learn as you are watching.
既然你是第一次,你可以边看边学。

● 条件状语从句

I will marry you **if that can atone for my mistake**.
如果那能够弥补我的过错,我会嫁给你。

Unit 5 状语从句

They are those who are never happy **unless they're running about doing things.**
他们是那种每天不找点事做就不开心的人。
If you are too tired, I won't insist on you trying them.
如果你太累了，我不会坚持让你去试一下。
You can live here **as long as you would like to.**
只要你愿意，你就可以住在这里。、

条件状语从句告诉我们主句动词所表示动作发生的条件。它描述主句动词所表示动作或状态发生的前提和条件：如果要有后者的存在必须先有前者的存在或出现。一般翻译成"如果……就……、只要……就……、除非……（否则）……"等。

As long as the girl sticks it out, she will get this job.
只要这个女孩坚持到底，她会得到这份工作的。
If we removed this part from the man, he would not be a man.
如果这个男人身上的这个特点没有了，他也就不能称之为人了。
In case he comes, let me know.
如果他来了，告诉我一声。

> 常用的连接条件状语从句的从属连词有：if, unless, as long as, in case, provided that（假如……）等。

☞思考：如果条件句表示的是一个根本不存在或是根本不可能实现的条件又或是只是自己的猜想，那应该怎样表示呢？想想这个句子应该怎样表述？"如果我要是公司老板，一定先解决这个问题。"

※注：条件句分为真实条件句和非真实条件句：当从句中的条件是真实的，有可能实现的时候，是真实条件句用陈述语气；当从句的条件与客观事实相反，没有可能实现，或只是某种假设与猜想或愿望时，是非真实条件句用虚拟语气。（参见"虚拟语气"）

● 方式状语从句

Do it **as I have told you.**
按照我曾经告诉你的那样做。
She speaks to her husband **as she orders her subordinates.**
她和自己的丈夫说话就像是命令自己的下属。
I don't want to see that **as if we forced him to do so.**
我不想看到那个样子，就好像是我们强迫他那样做似的。
My parents always allow me to do things **the way I would like to do them.**
我父母总是让我按照自己的意愿做任何事。

方式状语从句告诉我们主句动词所表示动作发生的方式,或是某个人的行为方式。它描述主句动词所表示动作或状态发生的方式。即后者的表现方式是前者描述的状态。一般翻译成"按照……、就像……等"。

My best friend enjoys every kind of food as I do.
我最好的朋友喜欢所有的食物,就像我一样。
I want to pass the exam as my parents has been expecting.
我想通过这次考试就像我父母一直期望的那样。
I will not publish my paper the way others do it.
我不会像其他人那样发表我的文章。

☞ 思考:上面例句中的从句中出现了几个 do,它们有什么作用?分别是什么意思?

> 常用的连接方式状语从句的从属连词有:as, as if, the way, as though 等。

● 结果状语从句

She is so famous that even some foreigners come for her.
她的名气很大,以至于一些外国人都慕名而来。
Johnson is such a good doctor that some patients would rather wait to see him.
约翰逊是一个很好的大夫以至于一些病人宁愿等着让他看病。
You'd better finish your paper by tonight so that we can hand it in tomorrow.
你最好今晚之前完成你的论文好让我们明天可以交稿。

结果状语从句告诉我们主句动词所表示动作发生之后导致的(或将会导致的)结果。它描述主句动词所表示动作或状态发生之后的结果。结果状语从句要放在主句的后面,一般翻译成"……以至于……、……结果……"等。

This is such a movie that everyone will be moved.
这部电影很棒,会让很多人感动。
The boss is so busy that few people can find him.
这位老板很忙以至于很少有人能找到他。
The journalist went there very early so that he got a good seat.
这个记者很早到了那里,所以找到了一个好位子。
The girl types so fast that the manager decided to hire her.
这个女孩打字很快,所以经理决定聘用她。

> 常用的连接结果状语从句的从属连词有:so…that, such…that, so that 等。

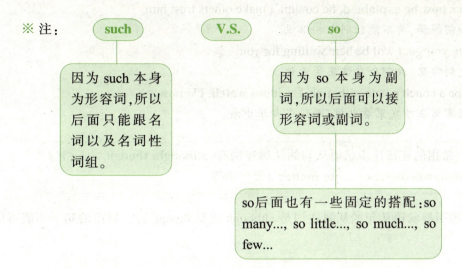

He is **so** <u>good</u> a doctor **that all the patients love him.**
He is **such** <u>a good doctor</u> **that all the patients love him.**
他是一个好大夫,所有病人都喜欢他。
The boy has **so** <u>many</u> friends **that he can meet some everywhere he goes.**
这个男孩有许多朋友,以至于无论他到哪儿都会遇到朋友。
The water is **so** <u>little</u> **that not all the people can have a drink.**
水太少了,不够所有人都喝一口。

● 让步状语从句

Although the boy broke the window, he didn't feel guilty at all.
虽然这个男孩子打破了窗玻璃,但是他没有一点歉疚的意思。
He wears a T-shirt **though it is very cold.**
天气虽然很冷可是他却穿了一件 T 恤衫。
Even if you can finish it on time, I will not recommend you.
即使你能够按时完成工作,我也不会推荐你。
Whether you believe it or not, I have sold my favorite watch.
不管你信还是不信,我都已经卖了那块我最喜欢的手表。

　　让步状语从句告诉我们一个和主句谓语动词所表示动作或状态在逻辑关系上相反的一个动作或状态。或者是从句的这个动作或状态会使得主句的描述更加引人注意。总之,通过让步状语从句的修饰和描述,我们会对主句的内容更加印象深刻。一般翻译成"虽然……但是、尽管……还……、即使……也……"等。

No matter how he explained, he couldn't make others trust him.
不管他如何解释，都不能让别人相信他。
Wherever you go, I will be here waiting for you.
无论你走到哪里，我都会在这里等着你。
I used to be a couch potato **although I seldom watch TV now.**
我过去经常窝在沙发里看电视，而现在却很少看。

> 常用的连接让步状语从句的从属连词有：although, though, even if / though, whether... or..., no matter +疑问词等。

※ 注：当引导状语从句的从属连词是 although 或是 though 时，后面的句子不能再用 but。

{ (×) **Although** I seldom watch TV now, **but** I used to be a couch potato.
  (√) **Although** I seldom watch TV now, I used to be a couch potato.
  虽然我现在很少看电视，但是以前我可是一个电视迷。

{ (×) **Though** I don't want to do that, **but** I prefer you to have a try.
  (√) **Though** I don't want to do that, I prefer you to have a try.
  虽然我不想做，我却想让你试一试。

☞ 思考：however 既可以作并列句的连词，也可以作从属连词引导让步状语从句，想想看它们之间有什么差异呢？

> 名词/形容词/副词+as+主语+谓语，主句…

※ 注：as 引导的倒装结构也可以用作让步状语从句。这里的倒装用部分倒装结构，而且置于 as 之前的名词前面不能加任何冠词。翻译成汉语为"虽然……但是……"。

Young as she is, the girl can take care of her parents.
这个女孩虽然年轻，但是她可以照顾自己的父母。
Hard as he worked, the young man could not make any progress.
这个年轻人虽然努力工作，但是却没有任何进展。
Child as Tom is, he can earn money for himself.
汤姆虽然是个孩子，但是他能自己挣钱。

Unit 5　状语从句

● 目的状语从句

I get up very early everyday **in order that I can catch the bus.**
我每天早晨很早起床是为了要赶公共汽车。
I made myself crouch **so that the kid could be heard.**
我蹲下来以便能听到这个小孩说什么。
You'd better take an umbrella **in case it rains.**
你最好带上伞以防下雨。
It is better to make an apologize **lest the others should get angry.**
你最好道歉以免别人生气。

　　目的状语从句告诉我们某个动作或状态发生或出现的目的。即从句所描述的动作或状态是主句所描述的动作或状态的目的，一般翻译成"以便……，以免……，……是为了……"等。目的状语从句中多用 will, can, could, might, may, should, would 等情态动词。

You must <u>not be late</u> **in order that you can** <u>leave a fine first impression</u> to them.
你一定不能迟到，为的是要给他们留下一个好的第一印象。
The country should <u>control its population</u> **so that it can** <u>make a development.</u>
国家控制人口增长，目的是要获得发展。
We <u>invited</u> the guests to our new apartment **in case they** <u>thought we were not sincere.</u>
我们邀请客人到我们的新居作客，以免他们认为我们没有诚意。

☞ 思考：在某种特定的场合中应该使用哪一种特定的状语从句呢？

> 　　常用的连接目的状语从句的从属连词有：so that..., in order that..., for fear (that)..., in case..., lest...等。

 重点及难点 (Key points)

● 时间状语从句和条件状语从句中不允许使用将来时态

　　※ 注：时间状语从句和条件状语从句不能使用将来时态，所以要用一般现在时来代替一般将来时，而用现在完成时来代替将来完成时。

After you finish your homework, you can do what you like to do.
你写完作业之后，可以做你喜欢做的事。

I will not leave **until the baby's mother comes back**.
我会一直等到孩子的妈妈回来才离开。
You can come **as long as you get the ticket**.
只要你拿到票就可以来了。
If it doesn't rain tomorrow, we will go fishing.
如果明天不下雨,我们就去钓鱼。
Provided that I have finished it by that time, you must keep your promise.
假如那个时间之前我已经完成工作,你必须履行诺言。

● until 和 till

① until 和 till 都表示"……直到……",即他们都表示的是一段时间,所以它们连接的主句中的动词必须是有延续性的。但是如果主句用的是否定形式,则动词既可以是延续性也可以是非延续性的,意思是"直至……才开始……"。
I fell into sleep until / till you came to knock at my door. (×)
I slept until / till you came to knock at my door. (√)
我一直在睡,直到你来敲门。
或者:你来敲门之前我一直在睡觉。
I didn't fall into sleep until / till you came back. (√)
直到你回来我才睡着。

② 如果把时间状语从句放在句首,那么我们多用 until 而通常不用 till。
Until you told me, I knew nothing about it.
你告诉我之前我对那件事一无所知。
Until everybody has gone, I have been busy with this report.
我一直在忙着弄这份报告,直到所有人都走了。

③ Not until... 放在句首引导时间状语从句的时候,主句要使用部分倒装。
Not until the children were dismissed, could the teacher have a rest.
直到所有的孩子都散了,老师才能休息一下。
Not until you came, would I tell you the truth.
你来了我才告诉你真相。

● 三个表示"一……就……"的固定搭配

① hardly / scarcely... when...
I had **hardly** entered the classroom **when** the bell rang.
我一走进教室铃声就响了。

The guest had **scarcely** arrived **when** the host came out to meet him.
客人一到主人就走出来迎接。

※ 注：**hardly / scarcely** 可以放在句首，这时从句要使用部分倒装。
Hardly had I finished the paper when the bell rang.
我刚一写完，铃就响了。
Scarcely had the boy came home when it began to rain.
这个男孩儿刚到家就下起了雨。

☞ 思考：试着把前两个句子也变成倒装句。

② **no sooner... than...**
I had **no sooner** heard her voice **than** I went out.
我一听到她的声音就走出去。
The patient had **no sooner** arrived **than** the doctor operated on him.
病人一到医生就立刻给他做手术。

※ 注：no sooner 也可以放在句首，这时从句同样要使用部分倒装。
No sooner had I come in than the man stopped his talking.
我刚一进来，那个男的就不说了。
No sooner had the baby seen his mother **than** he smiled.
这个婴儿一见到自己的妈妈就笑了。

同时需要注意的是，在①和②这两种表达方式中，几乎不用现在时态或将来时态。

☞ 思考：在这种表达中，no sooner 后面的动作和 than 后面的动作，哪一个更早发生呢？

③ **...as soon as...**
I went out **as soon as** I heard her voice.
我一听到她的声音就出去了。
I will send the book to you **as soon as** I receive the money.
我一收到钱就把书寄给你。

● 状语从句中的虚拟语气

使用状语从句来修饰主句的动作或是状态时，不要忘记虚拟语气的存在与应用。除了在条件状语从句中提到的非真实条件句，还有一些表现形式，一般来讲主要有以下几种：

① 方式状语从句中的虚拟语气：**as if / as though**
　　由 as if 或者 as though 引导方式状语从句时，其从句的谓语动词多用虚拟语气，即动词的过去式或过去完成式。

　　He spoke to us **as if** he **were** our teacher.
　　他跟我们说话就好像是我们的老师似的。
　　They talked as usual **as if** they **had not quarreled** with each other.
　　他们像平常那样聊着就好像之前根本没有吵过架。
　　The man told the story **as though** he **had experienced** it himself.
　　那个男的讲了一个故事就好像他曾经亲身经历过一样。
　　The boss ignored the facts **as though** they never **existed.**
　　老板对这些事实视而不见就好像事情根本没有发生过。

② 让步状语从句中的虚拟语气：**even if / even though**
　　由 even if 或者 even though 引导让步状语从句时，其从句的谓语动词多用虚拟语气，即动词的过去式或过去完成式。

　　Even if you **had bought** this, I would not accept.
　　即使你已经买了，我也不会要。
　　Even if you **knew** the boss, he would not allow that.
　　即使你认识老板，他也不会允许。
　　Even though I **had** money, I would not lend to you.
　　即便我有钱也不会借给你。
　　Even though you **had not come,** I would go.
　　即使你没来，我也要去。

③ 目的状语从句中的虚拟语气：**in case, lest, for fear that**
　　由 in case, lest, for fear that 引导目的状语从句时，其从句的谓语动词用虚拟语气，即"should + 动词原形"的形式。

　　You must keep the secret **lest** the others **(should) know** it.
　　你必须保守秘密，以免别人知道了。
　　You'd better take an umbrella **in case** it **(should) rain.**
　　你最好戴上伞，以防下雨。
　　I will remind you tomorrow **for fear that** you **(should) forget.**
　　明天我会提醒你，以免你忘了。

虚拟语气更为详细的用法参见"虚拟语气"。

应用 (Practice)

I. Use adverbial clause to make the following sentences more vivid.（给下面各句添加合适的状语从句使它们更加形象生动。）

1. I speak to them for some time at first.
2. He finally lent money to me.
3. He saw the whole process just now.
4. The actor is reluctant to say anything about it.
5. The assistant managed to finish the project.
6. You have to return it tomorrow morning.
7. I will not assign this task to you.

II. Try to use proper conjunctions to connect the two sentences.
（用合适的连词连接各题中的两个句子。）

1. The man will not come.
   The man doesn't want to be involved in this matter.
2. He is very strong.
   He would feel exhausted after a whole day's work.
3. Pass me the dictionary.
   Jack has used the dictionary.
4. The concert is a confusion, and the band doesn't play well.
   The band used to play well.
5. You can borrow my mobile phone.
   You return it to me tonight.
6. The thief got off the bus.
   The thief was caught by the police.
7. The speech was very boring.
   Everyone felt bored.
8. He refused to tell us.
   He would undertake the job.

III. Find sentences with adverbial clauses in the following paragraph and translate them into Chinese. （找出下面这段文字中带有状语从句的句子并把它们翻译成汉语。）

Hi! Remember me? (Just a joke!) I haven't written to you for at least six months, but that's not long enough for you to forget me! You haven't heard from me for such a long time because I have been really busy. When I wrote to you six months ago - last April, I think - I was going to the university full-time and studying anthropology. A lot of things have happened since then. Now I have a job in a shoe store. It isn't a bad job, but it isn't wonderful either. Every day, I fetch shoes from the back room for people to try on. I have met some pretty weird people since I started this job. A couple of weeks ago, a middle-aged man came into the store and wanted to try on some black leather loafers. I brought them, and he put them on. While he was walking around to see if they fit okay, he pulled from his pocket a little white mouse with pick eyes and asked for its opinion. When the mouse twitched its nose, the man said, "We'll take them."

IV. Could you make a dialogue or a passage which contains some sentences with adverbial clause?（用带有状语从句的句子编写一段对话或是一段文字。）

从句

I. In this section, there are 10 incomplete sentences. You are required to complete each one by deciding on the most appropriate word or words from the 4 choices marked A, B, C and D.

1. _____ is often the case, one third of the workers have over-fulfilled the production plan.
   A. What   B. This   C. That   D. As

2. Mr. Jones, _____ life was once very hard, is now very successful in his business.
   A. of him   B. his   C. whose   D. by whom

3. She got to know the young man very well _____ she had worked for so long.
   A. to whom   B. in whom   C. whom   D. with whom

4. This book is designed for the learners _____ native languages are not English.
   A. whose   B. which   C. who   D. what

5. The hotel _____ during the vacation was rather poorly managed.
   A. as I stayed   B. where I stayed   C. which I stayed   D. what I stayed

6. She wanted to know _____ child it was on the grass.
   A. that   B. whose   C. what   D. whom

7. This is the microscope _____ which we have had so much trouble.
   A. at   B. from   C. of   D. with

8. We were talking about the American tourist _____ we met during our trip to the Great wall.
   A. what   B. which   C. whose   D. whom

9. The old man has two daughters, _____ are doctors.
   A. both of them   B. both of whom
   C. both who   D. they both

10. On April 1st they flew to Beijing, _____ they stayed several days.
    A. when   B. where   C. which   D. there

11. The police asked the villagers if it was the place _____ they found the lost child.
    A. which   B. what   C. that   D. where

12. The days _____ you could travel without a passport are gone.
    A. of which   B. on which   C. in which   D. at which

13. There is no evidence _____ oil price will come down in the near future.
    A. which   B. that   C. where   D. as
14. What do you think of his suggestion _____ we all attend the meeting?
    A. which   B. whether   C. that   D. what
15. We were all excited at the news _____ our annual sales had more than doubled.
    A. which   B. that   C. it   D. what
16. With the introduction of the computer, libraries today are quite different from _____ they were in the past.
    A. that   B. what   C. which   D. those
17. He got a message from Miss Zhang _____ Professor Wang couldn't see him the following day.
    A. which   B. whom   C. that   D. what
18. _____ breaks the law will be punished sooner or later.
    A. Who   B. Someone   C. Anyone   D. Whoever
19. The news _____ the Chinese football team had won the match excited all of us.
    A. that   B. which   C. what   D. as
20. There is a nice-looking car over there. Peter wonders _____.
    A. it belongs to who   B. whom does it belong to
    C. whom it belongs to   D. who does it belong
21. The fact _____ Mary was late for the meeting again made me angry.
    A. that   B. why   C. what   D. which
22. It makes no difference to me _____ Mr. Smith will come or not.
    A. when   B. how   C. that   D. whether
23. The policeman saw the thief _____ he appeared on the street corner.
    A. not until   B. as long as   C. the moment   D. only if
24. You can't get a driver's license _____ you are at least sixteen years old.
    A. if   B. unless   C. when   D. though
25. The young man lost his job last month, but it wasn't long _____ he found a new position in my company.
    A. before   B. while   C. as   D. after
26. _____ you have any questions or needs, please contact the manager after 5:00 p.m. on weekdays.
    A. Because   B. Where   C. If   D. Through
27. When he went out, he would wear sunglasses _____ nobody would recognize him.
    A. so that   B. now that   C. as though   D. in case
28. _____ Susan gets onto the top of a tall building, she will feel very much frightened.
    A. Now that   B. Even though   C. Every time   D. Only if
29. _____ he is still working on the project, I don't mind when he will finish it.
    A. In case   B. As long as   C. Even if   D. As far as

30. Li Lei didn't meet the famous American professor _____ he was on holiday in America last year.
    A. unless   B. until   C. if   D. whether
31. She didn't go to the cinema last night, _____ she had to finish her term paper.
    A. as   B. if   C. till   D. though
32. We moved to London _____ we could visit our friends more often.
    A. even if   B. so that   C. in case   D. as if
33. The criminal didn't realize the value of freedom _____ he had lost it.
    A. if   B. as   C. while   D. until
34. I'll lend you my computer _____ you promise to take care of it.
    A. unless   B. as   C. while   D. if
35. Don't worry. _____ you work hard, you are sure to pass the exam.
    A. as much as   B. as well as   C. as soon as   D. as long as
36. The machine will continue to make much noise _____ we have it repaired.
    A. when   B. because   C. if   D. unless
37. It makes no differences to me _____ Mr. Smith will come or not.
    A. when   B. how   C. that   D. whether
38. There are two doors, one of which _____ to the living room and the other to the kitchen.
    A. leads   B. to lead   C. leading   D. led
39. The book is _____ more difficult than the one I recommended to you.
    A. very   B. rather   C. so   D. much
40. If you _____ smoking and drinking, your health will improve soon.
    A. gave up   B. give up   C. had given up   D. will give up
41. He bought an expensive coat _____ he had no job.
    A. unless   B. since   C. although   D. till
42. _____ the population is too large, the government has to take measures to control the birth rate.
    A. Although   B. Since   C. If   D. Until
43. You can drive your own car _____ you have passed the driving test.
    A. now that   B. even if   C. so that   D. as if
44. The harder I tried, _____ it seemed to solve that math problem.
    A. the possible   B. most possible
    C. the most possible   D. the more possible
45. Some people think _____ about their rights than they do about their responsibilities.
    A. so much   B. too much   C. much more   D. much too
46. The cost of traveling around the eight European countries can run as high _____ $2,000.
    A. to   B. as   C. by   D. for

47. Which do you think is _____ important, wealth or health?
   A. more   B. most   C. the more   D. the most
48. The _____ the proposal is considered, the worse it appears.
   A. carefully   B. much carefully   C. most carefully   D. more carefully
49. As Edison grew _____, he never lost his interest in science.
   A. the elder   B. elder   C. the oldest   D. older

II. **There are 10 incomplete statements here. You should fill in each blank with the proper form of the word given in the brackets.**

1. The more challenging the journey is, the (happy) _____ the young people will feel.
2. Those who are working in the Human Resources Department are (humorous) _____ than we expected.
3. There is a well-known proverb: "The more haste, the (little) _____ speed."
4. I'm the (little) _____ experienced of all the doctors here.
5. He knows even (little) _____ about the Olympic Games than I do.
6. John is the (clever) _____ student I have ever taught.
7. Every day the director is the (late) _____ person to leave the office.
8. One can jump (high) _____ on the moon than on the earth.
9. I want to rent a new apartment that is (comfortable) _____ than this one.

Unit 6 There be 句型
("There be" Sentence Pattern)

 导入 (Lead-in)

TASK:
上面这幅图是一间教室的一角。给我们介绍一下它,讲讲看这间教室里有什么东西?

 讲解 (Explanation)

● There be 句型概述

上面的四个句子分别告诉我们有四个人所做的事或是所处的状态:
There is a blackboard on the wall.
墙上有一面黑板。
There are 5 lovely kids in the classroom.
教室里有 5 个可爱的孩子。
There is a plant at the corner of the classroom.
教室角落处有植物。
There are some pictures on the wall too.
墙上还有一些画。

像上面这四个句子描述的,导入部分的图片所显示的教室里有很多东西:墙上有黑板、还有画、地上有乌龟、黑板上有数字、书架上有鱼缸和镜子、课桌上有书、书架里有书、墙角处有植物、鱼缸里有鱼,再有就是教室里有 5 个可爱的小朋友……,当你想告诉别人这些内容时就需要用到 there be 句型。

☞ 思考:如果我们用 have / has 来表示这种某地有什么东西可以吗?

> There be 在英语中陈述事物的客观存在,表示"有,存在"的意思。

在这个句型结构中,there 为引导词,本身并没有实际的意义。be 为谓语动词,真正的主语是 be 后面的名词。这个名词多是表示泛指或不定特指的名词或名词性词组。其后会有表示时间或地点的状语。所以如果想表达"在某个地方或某个时间有什么东西或是人存在",就使用这个句型:

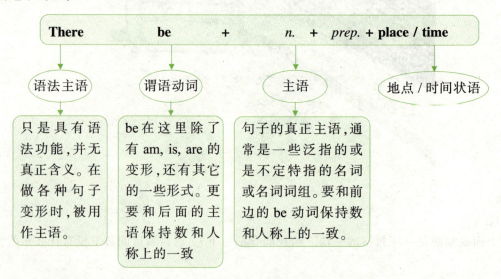

There is a shop across the street.
街对面有一家商店。

There are a lot of rumors about the actor on the Internet.
网上有很多关于那个演员的谣言。

There is nothing to tell you.
无可奉告。

There came plenty of strangers today.
今天来了很多陌生人。

There are a lot of fishes in the water.
水里有很多鱼。

※注：there be 句型中我们一般不使用进行时态或是完成进行时态。

☞ 思考：现实生活中，我们会在什么场合中使用 there be 句型呢？

★ **There be 句型主要表达下面三类意思：**

① There are some books on the shelf.
架子上有一些书。
There are five people in my office.
我的办公室里有五个人。

> 表示某个地方或某个时间有什么人或物存在。

② There is going to be a lecture of the famous professor this afternoon.
今天下午有一场这位知名教授的讲座。
There is only one person who has failed the exam.
只有一个人没有通过这次考试。

> 信息通知，报道或是预先安排。

③ There is too much wind in Beijing.
北京经常刮风。
It was rainy last night, and there was still a heavy rain this morning.
昨晚上下雨，今天早晨仍在下大雨。

> 天气现象。

☞ 思考：如何把 there be 句型变成疑问句或否定句呢？谓语和主语的位置关系应该怎样变化？

重点及难点 (Key points)

● **There be 句型的语法规则**

★ **There be 句型中的主谓一致：**

① 这个句型中的 be 动词要和他后面的名词或名词词组保持数以及人称的一致。
There *is a bird* in the sky.
天空中有一只鸟。（这句话的真正主语 a bird 是第三人称单数形式所以 be 动词用 is。）

57

There **are** *a flock of birds* in the sky.

天空中有一群鸟。(这句话的真正主语是 a flock of birds 是第三人称复数形式，所以 be 动词用 are。)

② 就近原则：当句子的真正主语是几个并列的名词或词组时，be 动词的形式与距离他最近的名词或词组(也就是第一个主语)保持数与人称的一致。

{ There **is** *a desk,* a chair and some people in this room.
  There **are** *some people,* a desk and a chair in this room.
  这间屋子里有一张桌子、一把椅子和一些人。}

{ There **is** *a purse,* two cards, a pair of glasses and a bunch of keys in the bag.
  There **are** *two cards,* a pair of glasses, a purse and a bunch of keys in the bag.
  这个包里有一个钱包、一副眼镜、两张卡和一串钥匙。}

在第一组句子中，第一个句子里，紧跟在 be 动词后面的是 a desk 为第三人称单数，所以 be 动词采用相应的形式 is；而第二个句子里，紧跟在 be 动词后面的换成是 some people 为第三人称复数，所以 be 动词也换用相应的形式 are。第二组句子是一样的，先是 is 后紧跟第三人称单数 a purse；再是 are 后紧跟第三人称复数 two cards。

★ **There be 句型的时态：**

There be 句型中除了不能用进行时态或完成进行时态，基本可以使用任何一种时态来表达不同的含义。

There **is** a movie theater on the campus. (一般现在时)
校园里有一间电影院。
There **was** a movie theater on the campus. (一般过去时)
校园里曾经有一间电影院。
There **is going to be** a movie theater on the campus. (一般将来时)
校园里将会有一间电影院。
There **has been** a movie theater on the campus. (现在完成时)
校园里已经有一间电影院了。
There **have been** great changes in the city in the past twenty years. (现在完成时)
在过去的 20 年间，这个城市发生了巨大的变化。

可见，there be 句型的时态变化就是 be 动词的时态变化。

☞ 思考：体会一下不同的时态给这个句型的含义带来什么不同的变化？

Unit 6　There be 句型

★ **There be 句型的转换：**

> 否定形式：

① There be 句型的 be 动词后或是助动词后加 not：

There **are not** any pens in the pencil box.（be+not）
铅笔盒里没有钢笔。

There **is not** a tree in the yard.（be+not）
院子里没有树。

There **will not be** any rain for a long time.（助动词+not+be）
很长一段时间不会有雨。

There **have not been** any changes here these years.（助动词+not+be）
这个地方这些年来没有任何变化。

There **was not** a meeting yesterday.（be+not）
昨天没有会。

② there be 句型的主语前加 no：

There are **no** pens in the pencil box.
铅笔盒里没有钢笔。

There are **no** trees in the yard.
院子里没有树。

There will be **no** rain for a long time.
很长一段时间不会有雨。

There have been **no** changes here these years.
这个地方这些年来没有任何变化

There were **no** meetings yesterday.
昨天没有会。

There was **no** water in this village.
这里以前没有水。

> 疑问形式：

① 一般疑问句：
There be 句型的一般疑问句形式就是把 be 动词前置或是助动词前置，回答用 "yes" 或 "no"，后接简略的答句。

{ ——Is there a tree in the yard?
{ ——Yes, there is. / No, there isn't.
——院子里有树吗？
——有。/ 没有。

59

{ ——Are there any pens in the pencil box?
　——Yes, there are. / No, there aren't.
　——铅笔盒里有钢笔吗?
　——有。/ 没有。

{ ——Will there be any rain in the following days?
　——Yes, there will. / No, there won't.
　——今后几天有雨吗?
　——有。/ 没有。

{ ——Have there been any changes in your hometown recently?
　——Yes, there have. / No, there haven't.
　——最近你们家乡发生什么变化了吗?
　——有变化。/ 没变化。

{ ——Was there a meeting yesterday?
　——Yes, there was. / No, there wasn't.
　——昨天开会了吗?
　——开了。/ 没开。

② 特殊疑问句:
There be 句型的特殊疑问句形式主要是用 how many 和 how much 提问。形式为:
How many / much + *n.* + be + there + time / place...
How many students are there in the university?
这所大学里有多少学生?
How many provinces are there in China?
中国有多少个省?
How much money is there in your wallet?
你的钱包里有多少钱?
How much water is there on earth in the desert?
沙漠里到底有多少水?

③ 反义疑问句:
There be 句型的反义疑问句形式需要把 be 动词或是助动词提前，其后跟语法主语 there。
There **is** a person over there, **isn't there**?
那边有一个人,对吗?
There **won't** be any evidence, **will there**?
不会有任何证据,是吗?

There have been no letters from her for a month, **have there**?
一个星期都没有她的信了，是吗？
There was nothing serious, **was there**?
没有什么严重的事，对吗？
There are still a lot of opportunities, **aren't there**?
还是有很多机会的，对吗？

> 反义疑问句后面的附加疑问部分的 be 动词或是助动词要和前面陈述部分的谓语部分状态相反——前面是肯定，后面是否定；前面是否定，后面是肯定。

☞ 思考：there be 句型中的 be 动词可以用其他词来代替吗？

● be 动词的一些特殊形式

> be 动词除了用 am, is, are 之外还有一些特殊的谓语动词也可以用在这里。如：**live**, **stand**, **exist**, **appear**, **come**, **go**, **remain**, **seem to**, **appear to**, **be likely to**, **happen to** 等。

Once upon a time, **there lived** a king and a queen near the sea.
很久以前，离海不远住着一位国王和一位王后。
There seems to be some misunderstanding between us.
你我之间好像有一些误会。
There exist a lot of beautiful creatures in the nature.
在大自然中，存在着很多美丽的生物。
There stands the girl I have recommended to you.
我跟你推荐过的那个女孩站在那儿。
There happened to be someone nearby.
碰巧附近有人。

● There be 句型和情态动词搭配

There be 句型可以和各种情态动词搭配使用，表达不同的语气。参照"情态动词"一节。
There might be some money left in my bag.
我包里可能会剩下一些钱。
There must be something wrong with the computer.
这台电脑肯定是出了什么问题。
There should be ten people at this table.
这张桌子应该坐十个人。

There *used to be* a lot of trees along the road.
过去这里沿路有很多树。

☞ 思考：上面各个句子中的情态动词分别给每个句子增加了什么样的不同语气呢？

● **There be 句型的非谓语形式**

★ **There to be ... V.S. There being...**

There to be ...

① there to be 一般是作某些动词的宾语，常用的有：expect, want, like, hate, prefer 等。

I *expect* **there to be** some progress in your study.
我期望你的学习能有所进步。

I don't *want* **there to be** any misunderstanding between you two.
我不想你们两个之间有任何误会。

I *prefer* **there to be** some time for me to have a break.
我宁愿有一些时间可以让我喘口气。

② 用在 It be + *adj.* + for...后面。

It is important for **there to be** laws in a society.
一个社会中有法律的存在是很重要的。

It was impossible for **there to be** any extra money just two years ago.
就是两年前，有一点余钱都是不可能的。

It is wonderful for **there to be** some pictures on the wall.
墙上有几幅画很棒。

There being...

① there being 要作介词后的宾语。

I have been dreaming *of* **there being** so much money.
我一直梦想着会有这么多钱。

We are talking *about* **there being** too much work.
我们在谈论工作太多了。

Have you heard *of* **there being** an opportunity to go to France in our company?
你有没有听说我们公司有一个去法国的机会？

※注：介词 for 后面要跟 there to be 的形式。

The woman has been waiting *for* **there to be** a man who loves her truly.
这个女人一直在等着有一个男人真心爱自己。

The man never cares *for* **there to be** too much criticism.
这个男人根本不在意有太多的批评。

They fight *for* **there to be** more justice and happiness.
他们为有更多的公平与幸福而战。

② 作状语。

There being nobody coming, I will go.
因为没有人来，我要走了。

There being nothing to do, you can do whatever you like.
因为没有事做，你就可以做你喜欢的事。

● 其他

★ There is no...

这种用法都是在一些固定的搭配中使用：
There is no point / use / good + doing ... , 甚至可以直接在 no 后面加 doing。

There is no point finding so many data right now.
此时此刻找这么多数据没有意义。

There is no good arguing with your boss.
和你的老板吵架没有好处。

There is no use reciting so many words without using them practically.
不实际应用，只是背这么多单词没有用处。

There is no denying we will be responsible for this accident.
无可否认我们要为这次事故负责任。

★ There be 句型和 have 的区别：

There be 句型讲的是某地有某物 / 人，强调的是物或人的位置关系。而 have 讲的是某地/人拥有什么东西，强调的是所有关系。

There is a green bag on the desk.
强调 bag 在 desk 上："桌上有一个绿色的书包。"

I **have** a green bag.
强调 bag 是属于 I 的："我有一个绿色的书包。"

There is an emergency building in the hospital.
强调急诊楼的位置在医院里："这所医院里有一栋急诊大楼。"

The hospital **has** an emergency building and an office building.
强调医院对急诊楼和办公楼的拥有："这所医院有一栋急诊大楼和一栋办公楼。"

应用 (Practice)

I. Fill in the blanks with the proper forms of "be" or other verbs. （用"be"或者其他动词的适当形式填空。）

1. There _____ a popular belief among parents that they should make their kids receive the best education.
2. There _____ no chance of a mix-up, and their growth would be normal.
3. On the Internet itself, there _____ more detailed instructions for writing appropriate instructions and for writing appropriate e-mail messages recently.
4. On Christmas, there _____ something filled in your stocking.
5. There _____ some furniture in his room.
6. There _____ a big mountain just before our village.
7. It must be very cold tomorrow for there _____ a snow tonight.
8. There _____ some good news and valuable reports.
9. Have you ever thought of there _____ some changes in your life?
10. There _____ some reason why he left without telling anybody.

II. Change the following sentences according to the requests. （按要求改写下列句子。）

1. There are few kids under 3 in this kindergarten. （否定句）
2. In the United States, there are about 140,000 commercial fishermen. （对划线部分提问）
3. There can be some journalists taking cameras. （一般疑问句）
4. There exist hot arguments over this suggestion. （反义疑问句）
5. There are a lot of old women and children left in this village. （添加情态动词）

III. Translate the following sentences into Chinese or English. （中英文互译。）

1. If you live in debt, there is no point considering investing in stocks.
2. If someone got hold of your private information, there is no limit to what damage can be done.
3. There is no doubt that professional and vocational studies have become increasingly popular in our country.
4. Wasn't there a letter from an old friend?
5. Where there is no product yet meeting a need, the opportunities are unlimited.
6. 从前有一个人，他有一个儿子并且非常爱他。
7. 中欧之间没有直接的利益冲突。
8. 门铃响了，有人叫门。
9. 针对这个问题，仍然存在很多的怀疑。
10. 说多少话对这个老顽固来说都没有意义。

IV. Try to describe the environment around you. （描述你周围的环境。）

Unit 7　强调句 (Emphatic Sentences)

导入 (Lead-in)

在说话或者写文章的时候有什么方法可以突出强调某个词、词组或者句子呢？

☞ 思考：看看下面的句子，想想斜体部分的词在句子中起什么作用。

It was because he'd never had the opportunity *that* John hadn't learned to drive.
约翰没有学习驾驶，是因为他没机会学。

He *does* go to school every day.
他确实每天都去上学了。

He *himself* had finished the job when they came into their factory.
当他们到工厂的时候，他已经自己完成了工作。

It was Chairman of the committee *that* we elected her.
我们选她当的是委员会的主席。

{ *It was not until* they finished all of their work *that* they went to bed.
{ *Not until* they finished all of their work *did* they go to bed.
他们完成了所有的工作以后才上床睡觉。

讲解 (Explanation)

● It is/ was... that/ who 强调句

It was a bunch of flowers *that* he gave her as a birthday present.
他送她的生日礼物是一束花。

65

It is with their help **that** we have achieved all this.
正是有了他们的帮助，我们才能取得所有的一切。
It was Xiao Wang **who/ that** first put forward the idea.
是小王第一个提出了这个想法。
It is blue **that** we've painted the doors.
我们把门漆成的是蓝色。
It was because the water had risen **that** they could not cross the river.
正是因为水涨了，他们没有渡过河去。

> It is/ was + 被强调部分 + that/who/whom + 其他成分
> 这个句型可以强调除谓语动词外的一切句子成分。
> 强调主语，指人时引导词可使用 who 或 that；
> 强调宾语，指人时引导词可用 whom 或 that；
> 被强调部分不指人时，在任何情况下都只用 that。
> 动词使用 is 还是使用 was 取决于谓语动词的时态。现在时和将来时用 is，过去时用 was。

☞ 思考：前面句子中强调的都是什么成分？

● 反身代词强调

You should go and apologize to the customer **yourself.**
你应该亲自去向客户道歉。
I want to speak to the manager **himself,** not to his secretary.
我要同经理本人谈，而不是同他的秘书谈。

> 使用反身代词表示强调，意为"亲自"，"独自地"。在句中的位置比较灵活，可以跟在强调的词后，也可以放在句末。

● 助动词强调

He said that he would come and **did** come.
他说他要来，他果真来了。
Do be careful.
一定要仔细。
Martin **does** know how to become popular among his classmates.
马丁的确知道如何得到同学的欢迎。

> 什么样的助动词可以用于强调？强调什么部分？

Unit 7　强调句

* do 作为助动词表示强调,用于肯定句或祈使句中,意为"确实"、"真的"、"务必"。
* 此种强调只有 do, does 和 did, 没有其他形式,只能强调一般现在时和一般过去时的谓语动词。
* 过去时的动词强调要用 did, 其后的谓语动词用原形,不要继续用过去式,同样 does 后也不要继续使用单数的谓语动词,而使用动词原形。

● not until 结构强调

He **didn't** go to bed **until** ten o'clock.
直到 10 点他才睡觉。
(变为强调句式:)
It was **not until** ten o'clock that he went to bed.
Not until ten o'clock **did** he went to bed.

not until 本身就是否定结构, until 后的句子中还可以使用否定结构吗?

Li Ming **didn't** watch TV **until** he finished his homework.
李明做完作业后才看电视。
(变为强调句式:)
It was **not until** Li Ming finished his homework **that** he watched TV.
Not until he finished his homework **did** Li Ming watch TV.

* 因为句型中 It is (was) not until 已经是否定句了,that 后面的从句要用肯定句,不能再用否定句了。
* Not until 放句首时,主句部分倒装。

● 完全倒装表强调

Then came the chairman.
那时主席来了。
Here **is** your letter.
你的信。
There **goes** the bell.
铃响了。

什么叫做完全倒装?

> 完全倒装就是整个谓语置于主语之前。

> 当 **here, there, now, then, in, out, up, down, away** 等表示趋向的副词置于句首,且谓语动词是 **be, come, go, lie, run, rush** 等表示来去或状态的动词时,句子完全倒装。

● 部分倒装表强调

> 什么是部分倒装?

> 部分倒装就是谓语中的一部分,即系动词、助动词或情态动词提到主语之前。

1) *Never* **have** I seen such a performance.
   我从未看过如此糟糕的表演。
   Seldom **does** she go to see his aunt in the countryside.
   她很少去看望住在乡下的阿姨。
   By no means **can** you talk him into buying the lottery.
   你绝对没法说服他买彩票。

> 当否定词或含有否定词的短语,如 **no, not, never, seldom, little, hardly, scarcely, rarely, neither, nor, no sooner, nowhere, at no time, in no way, by no means** 等放在句首时,句子部分倒装。

2) *Only* in this way **can** you learn English well.
   只有那样,你才能学好英语。
   Only then **did** I realize I have made a big mistake.
   在那时,我才意识到自己犯了大错。

> **Only** + 副词/介词短语/状语从句置于句首时,句子部分倒装。

3) *So small* **was** the mark that I could hardly see it.
   这个标记太小了,我几乎看不见。
   Tom can speak French. *So* **can** Jack.
   汤姆会讲法语,杰克也会。

> **so** + 形容词/副词放在句首时,句子部分倒装;so 表示"也",且放在句首时,句子也部分倒装。

※ 注：当 so 引出的句子用以对上文内容加以证实或肯定时,不用倒装结构。so 这时的意思为"确实如此"。

Tom asked me to go to play football and <u>so I did</u>.
汤姆邀我去踢球,我去了。
It's raining hard. <u>So it is.</u>
雨下的很大。是的。

4) **Young** as he is, he knows a lot.
他尽管很年轻,但是他知道很多。
Scientist as he is, he wants to learn more.
尽管他已经是科学家了,他还想学更多的东西。

> as 引导的让步状语从句倒装：
> 形容词 / 名词(不带冠词) + as + 主语 + 系动词 be

重点及难点 (Key points)

● 强调句中 that 的省略

> 在 It is/was...that/who 强调句中，如果强调的是宾语，则可以省略 that/who。

Was it *her* **(that)** you were talking about?
你们正在谈论的是她吗？
It is not *him* **(who)** you are looking for.
你们要找的不是他。
It was *a new dictionary* **(that)** my father sent to me.
父亲给我的是本新字典。

> 如果强调的是时间状语或地点状语,that 也可以省略。

It was in that bookstore **(that)** I came across the book.
在那家书店我见到了那本书。
It was only yesterday **(that)** we first met.
只是在昨天我们才第一次会面。

应用 (Practice)

1. It was with great joy _____ he received the news that his long lost son would soon return home.
   A. as   B. that   C. so   D. for
2. _____ she first heard of the man referred to as a specialist.
   A. That was from Stephen   B. It was Stephen whom
   C. It was from Stephen that   D. It was Stephen that
3. In spite of all you say, I _____ think I am right.
   A. do really   B. did really   C. really do   D. really did
4. It was from my grandparents _____ I learned a lot.
   A. who   B. whom   C. that   D. which
5. It is the ability to do the job _____ matters not where you come from or what you are.
   A. one   B. that   C. what   D. if
6. _____ is it _____ has made Peter _____ he is today?
   A. What, that, that   B. That, that, what
   C. What, what, that   D. What, that, what
7. _____ people found out the behavior of electricity.
   A. Through experiment that   B. Through experiment it was
   C. It was through that experiment   D. It was through experiment that
8. It was not until she arrived in class _____ realized she had forgotten her book.
   A. and she   B. when   C. she   D. that she
9. It was not _____ midnight that they discovered the children were not in their beds.
   A. before   B. at   C. after   D. until
10. Not until Columbus discovered America _____ to Europe.
    A. bananas were brought   B. bananas brought
    C. are banana brought   D. were bananas brought
11. It was in that small room _____ they worked hard and dreamed of better days to come.
    A. where   B. in which   C. which   D. that
12. His mother had talked to him for two hours while he was watching TV, but _____.
    A. a little did he hear   B. little did he hear
    C. little heard he   D. a little heard he
13. "We have to stop talking here. Listen, _____!"
    "Hurry up, or we'll be late."
    A. There goes the bell   B. There does the bell go
    C. There the bell goes   D. Goes the bell there

14. I received his mother's telephone call at eleven. _____ that he was badly hurt in an accident yesterday.
    A. Then did I know   B. Only then I knew
    C. Only then did I know   D. Only then knew I

15. By no means _____ to our plan for the trip.
    A. will she agree   B. she will agree
    C. agrees she   D. will agree she

16. Little Tom is an orphan. _____, he has to make a living by himself.
    A. A child as he is   B. Child as he is
    C. Child as is he   D. A child though he is

17. Mother told Rose to buy some sugar in the supermarket and _____.
    A. so she did   B. she so did
    C. so did she   D. she did such

18. If you go to his birthday party next Friday, _____.
    A. so do I   B. so will I
    C. nor do I   D. nor will I

Unit 8　词类和句子成分(Word Class and Elements of Sentences)

导入 (Lead-in)

每个单词有什么不同的作用？是否有自己的类别？句中分别承担什么作用呢？

☞ 思考：看看下面句中的单词,其作用都有什么异同？

The shop stays open till midnight.
这家商店一直开到子夜。

John became a professor but his wife remained a saleswoman.
约翰当上了教授,而他太太仍然是个售货员。

I've decided to retire next year, but you won't have been told that yet, I suppose.
我决定明年退休,但是我想你还没有听说此事。

The general touched him on the head kindly.
将军轻轻地摸了摸他的头。

讲解 (Explanation)

　　英语中所有的词汇可以分为十大类,每类词汇在句子中都有其特定的位置和作用,因此分清每一个单词的词类对于学好英语具有非常关键的意义。

Unit 8　词类和句子成分

● 词类

名词（Nouns）	表示人或事物的词(包括专有名词和普通名词). 在句中可作主语、表语、补语、定语、同位语。 如： teacher, student, book
数词 (Numbers)	表示数量和顺序的词。在句中可作主语、表语、宾语、定语、同位语。如：eight, first, twenty
代词 (Pronouns)	代替名词和数词的词。 如：she, he, one .
动词 (Verbs)	表示动作或状态的词，在句中可作谓语。如：run, make, look.
形容词 (Adjectives)	表示人或事物的性质或状态的词，可作表语、补语、定语、同位语。如：beautiful, good, fantastic, excellent
副词 (Adverbs)	表示动作特征或形状特征，修饰动词，形容词，副词的词。可作表语、状语。 如：slowly, much, fast.
冠词 (Articles)	与名词连用，是起说明人或事物的作用的词。如：the, a, an.
介词 (Prepositions)	通常置于名词和代词（宾格）之前，表示名词和代词与其他词的关系。如：in, on, about.
连词 (Conjunctions)	连接词与词或者句子与句子的词。如：and, but, because.
感叹词 (Interjections)	是表示说话人的感情或语气的词。如：oh, hey.

☞ 思考：有没有词同时属于好几种词类呢？

● 句子成分

During the 1990s, **American country music** has become more and more popular.(名词)
20世纪90年代，美国乡村音乐变得越来越流行。
We often speak English in class.(代词)
我们经常在班里说英语。
One-third of the students in this class are girls.(数词)
班里三分之一的学生是女孩。
To swim in the river is a great pleasure.(不定式)
在河里游泳有很大的乐趣。
Smoking does harm to the health.(动名词)
吸烟有害健康。
The rich should help the poor.(名词化的形容词)
富人应该帮助穷人。
When we are going to have an English test has not been decided.(主语从句)
我们还没决定什么时候考英语考试。
It is necessary **to master a foreign language**.(it 作形式主语，真正的主语为后面的不定式)
掌握一门外语非常重要。

> 不同词类的词在句中都有不同的作用，在句中它们都作什么成分呢？

> 主语(subjects)：表示句子描述的是"谁"或"什么"，是谓语的陈述对象。通常由名词、代词、不定式、动名词或从句担任。

☞ 思考：主语只能由名词性成分构成吗？

✳ ✳ ✳ ✳ ✳ ✳ ✳ ✳

We **study** English.
我们学习英语。
He **lives** in Shanghai.
他住在上海。

> 谓语(Predicates)：说明主语的动作或状态，由动词或动词短语担任。

☞ 思考：英语的一句话中可以有几个谓语动词？

✳ ✳ ✳ ✳ ✳ ✳ ✳ ✳

Our teacher of English is an **American**.(名词)
我们英语老师是美国人。
Is it **yours**?(代词)
是你的吗？

> 什么词类可以充当表语？

The weather has turned **cold**.(形容词)
天气已经变冷了。
The speech is **exciting**.(分词)
演讲令人兴奋。
Three times seven is **twenty one**.(数词)
三乘以七是二十一。
His job is **to teach English**.(不定式)
他的工作是教英语。
His hobby(爱好) is **playing football**.(动名词)
他的爱好是打篮球。
The machine must be **out of order**.(介词短语)
这机器肯定是出问题了。
Time is up. The class is **over**.(副词)
时间到了。下课。
The truth is **that he has never been abroad**.(表语从句)
事实是他从来没有出过国。

> 表语(Predicatives)：说明主语的性质或特征，由名词、形容词、副词、不定式、动名词或从句担任。

74

> 切记：表语这一成分是汉语中所没有的，所以在学习使用的时候，一定要注意它的结构、变化。

* * * * * * * * *

They went to see **an exhibition**(展览)yesterday.(名词)
昨天他们去看展览了。
The heavy rain prevented **me** from coming to school on time.(代词)
大雨使我没能准时来到学校。
How many dictionaries do you have? I have **five**.(数词)
你有几本字典？我有五本。
They helped **the old** with their housework yesterday.(名词化形容词)
他们昨天帮助老年人做家务。
He pretended **not to see me.**(不定式短语)
他装着看不见我。
I enjoy **listening to popular music.**(动名词短语)
我喜欢听流行音乐。
I think(that)**he is fit for his office.**(宾语从句)
我认为他适合他的职位。

> **宾语(Objects)**：表示及物动词或短语的对象或内容，由名词、代词、不定式、动名词或从句担任。

I give **you a piece of paper.**
我给你一张纸。
They made **him the chairman of the committee.**
他们选他为委员会的主席。

> 这句话中怎么有两个宾语呢？都有什么区别？

> 宾语种类：
> (1) 双宾语（间接宾语＋直接宾语），如：Lend me your dictionary, please.
> (2) 复合宾语（宾语＋宾补），如：They elected him their monitor.

☞ 思考：什么叫做直接宾语，什么叫做间接宾语？

* * * * * * * * *

Guilin is a **beautiful** city.(形容词)
桂林是一座美丽的城市。

China is a **developing** country; America is a **developed** country.(分词)
中国是发展中国家,美国是发达国家。

There are thirty **women** teachers in our school.(名词)
我们学校有三十名女教师。

His rapid progress in English made **us** surprised.(代词)
他在英语方面的快速进步使我们惊奇。

Our monitor is always the first **to enter the classroom.**(不定式短语)
我们班长总是第一个到达教室。

The **teaching** plan for next term has been worked out.(动名词)
他下学期的教学计划已经做出来了。

He is reading an article **about how to learn English.**(介词短语)
他正在读一本如何学英语的文章。

> 定语(Attributes):修饰或限定名词或代词,由形容词、代词、不定式、动名词或从句担任。

☞ 思考:不同的词作定语,位置如何呢?

* * * * * * * *

His father named him **Dongming**.(名词)
他爸爸叫他东明。

They painted their boat **white**.(形容词)
他们把船漆成白色。

Let the fresh air **in**.(副词)
让新鲜空气进来。

You mustn't force him **to lend his money to you**.(不定式短语)
你不能强迫他把钱借给你。

We saw **her entering the room**.(现在分词)
我们看到她走进房间。

We found everything **in the lab** in good order.(介词短语)
我们发现试验室里非常整齐。

We will soon make our city **what your city is now**.(从句)
我们很快就会把我们的城市建造得跟你们的城市一样。

> 补语(Complements):补充说明主语或宾语,由形容词、名词、代词担任。

☞ 思考:主语补足语和宾语补足语有什么区别?

* * * * * * * *

Light travels most **quickly**.(副词及副词性词组)
光速最快。
He has lived **in the city for ten years**.(介词短语)
他在这座城市已经住了十年了。
He is proud **to have passed the national college entrance examination**.(不定式短语)
他通过了高考很骄傲。
He is in the room **making a model plane**.(分词短语)
他正在房间做模型飞机。
Wait a **minute**.(名词)
等一下。
Once you begin, you must continue.(状语从句)
你一旦开始了,就必须继续。

> **状语(Adverbials)**：修饰动词、形容词、副词或整个句子。通常由副词、不定式、分词或从句担任。

☞ 思考：状语有分类吗？都有些什么样的种类呢？

※ ※ ※ ※ ※ ※ ※ ※

How about meeting again **at six**?（时间状语）
六点钟再见面如何?
Last night she didn't go to the dance party **because of the rain**.(原因状语)
昨天晚上因为下雨她没去参加聚会。
I shall go there **if it doesn't rain**.(条件状语)
如果不下雨,我会去那儿。
Mr. Smith lives **on the third floor**.(地点状语)
史密斯先生住在第三层。
She put the eggs into the basket **with great care**.(方式状语)
她很小心地把鸡蛋放进篮子里。
She came in **with a dictionary in her hand**.(伴随状语)
她手里拿着本字典走进来。
In order to catch up with the others, I must work harder.(目的状语)
为了赶上别人,我必须努力工作。
He was so tired **that he fell asleep immediately**.(结果状语)
他很劳累立刻睡着了。
She works very hard **though she is old**.(让步状语)
她虽然年纪大了,还是很努力工作。
I am taller **than he is**.(比较状语)
我比他高。

> 状语的类别：时间状语、原因状语、条件状语、地点状语、方式状语、伴随状语、目的状语、结果状语、让步状语与比较状语等等。

✲ ✲ ✲ ✲ ✲ ✲ ✲ ✲

This is Mr.Zhou, **our headmaster.**
这是周先生，我们的校长。

> 同位语(Appositives)：对前面的名词，代词做进一步的解释，由名词、形容词担任。

✲ ✲ ✲ ✲ ✲ ✲ ✲ ✲

To be honest, I don't agree with you.
我实话，我不同意你的观点。

> 插入语(Parenthesis)：对一句话做一些附加性的解释。

重点及难点 (Key points)

● 表语

和汉语不一样的就是英语中存在表语。表语表明主语"是什么/怎么样"，由名词、形容词、副词、介词、不定式或相当于名词或形容词的词或短语表示。它存在于系动词后面。
如：He is sleeping 中 is 是系动词，所以 sleeping 在这里为表语。

● 宾补和双宾语的区别

宾语与补充的内容可以形成逻辑上的主谓关系，而双宾成分不能互为主谓关系。
He made the boy laugh.　　　the boy—laugh 主谓关系　宾补
She bought me a pen.　　　me—a pen 无主谓关系　双宾

应用 (Practice)

I. **Form nouns by adding suffixes to the following.**(通过增加后缀把下列词变成名词。)

depend	explain	form	conclude	inform	move	mean
govern	graduate	similar	confuse	pay	agree	advertise
announce	add	decide	useful	attract	mix	

II. Form adjectives by adding suffixes to the following. （通过增加后缀把下列词变成形容词。）

science   success   response   color   nation   revolution
addition   help   person   vary   education meaning
accept   use   wood   act

III. Form the opposites of the following by adding prefixes to them. （增加前缀把下列词变成反义词。）

agree   practical   dependent   cover   complete   order
happy   formal   possible   active   certain   charge
honest   polite

IV. Point out the word classes and elements of sentences of the words. （指出句中词的词性和充当的句子成分。）

1. The students got on the school bus.
2. He handed me the newspaper.
3. I shall answer your question after class.
4. What a beautiful Chinese painting!
5. They went hunting together early in the morning.
6. His job is to train swimmers.
7. He took many photos of the palaces in Beijing.
8. There is going to be an American film tonight.
9. He is to leave for Shanghai tomorrow.
10. His wish is to become a scientist.
11. He managed to finish the work in time.
12. Tom came to ask me for advice.
13. He found it important to master English.
14. Do you have anything else to say?
15. To be honest, your pronunciation is not so good.
16. Would you please tell me your address?
17. He sat there, reading a newspaper.
18. It is our duty to keep our classroom clean and tidy.
19. He noticed a man enter the room.
20. The apples tasted sweet.

V. Point out the subject, predicate and object of the sentences. （指出下列句子的主语、谓语和宾语。）

I hope you are very well. I'm fine, but tired. Right now it is the summer vacation and I'm helping my Dad on the farm. August is the hottest month here. It is the time of year for the rice harvest, so every day I work from dawn until dark. Sometimes we go on working after dark by the lights of our tractors. We grow rice in the south of the States, but in the north where it is colder they grow wheat. We have a lot of machines on the farm. Although the farm is large, my Dad has only two men working for him. But he employs more men for the harvest. My brother takes care of the vegetable garden. It doesn't often rain in the summer here. As a result, we have to water the vegetable garden. Every evening we pump water from a well. It then runs along channels to different parts of the garden.

VI. Point out the attributes, adverbials and complements of the sentences. (指出下例句子的定语和状语。)

Most Saturday evenings there is a party, even at harvest time. These parties often make us very happy. We cook meat on an open fire outside. It's great! Americans eat a lot of meat—too much in my opinion. Some of my friends drink beer. I don't, because I have to drive home after the party. In your letter you asked about the time in different areas of the States. There are five different time areas in the States. In my state we are fourteen hours behind Beijing time. How many different time areas do you have in China? Well, I must stop and get some sleep. Please give my best regards to your parents.

Unit 9　名词的数和主谓一致 (Number System of Nouns and Subject-Verb Concord)

导入 (Lead-in)

下列句中名词形式有些什么样的变化，主语和谓语的变化又有什么样的联系？

In the *photos*, we can see the *Negroes* are eating *tomatoes* and *potatoes*.
I like these *dishes* but the *cup* for tea *is* too small.

看看下列句子，考虑一下他们是否存在单复数的变化和主谓一致的问题：
My child has no intention of spending a vacation with me.
我的孩子不想与我一起度假。
The only people who are interested in the book *seem* to be lawyers.
对这本书唯一感兴趣的好像是律师。
Billiards is becoming more and more popular in some cities.
桌球在一些城市里越来越受欢迎。

讲解 (Explanation)

● 可数名词

什么叫可数名词(countable nouns)？

能用数目计算的事物的名词叫可数名词(countable nouns)。大多数可数名词的复数形式在单数形式后加 s 或 es 构成。

☞ 思考：可数名词的单复数形式是如何变化的？

可数名词复数的一般形式

可数名词复数的一般形式在词尾加 s	girls, desks
s, x, ch, sh 结尾的名词在词尾加 es	classes, boxes, watches, brushes
辅音字母+y 结尾的名词，变 y 为 i 加 es	cities, babies
以 o 结尾的名词+s	photos, pianos, kilos, radios
以 o 结尾的名词+es	heroes, potatoes, tomatoes
名词以 f, fe 结尾时，变 f, fe 为 ve 加 s	knives, wolves, wives, lives, leaves

☞ 思考：可数名词有没有特殊的变化形式？

有些名词单复数同形	aircraft（飞行器），deer（鹿），sheep, fish, Chinese, Japanese, means（方法），series（系列）
集合名词只有复数形式	people, police, cattle（牛的总称），clothes, trousers, shoes, glasses(眼镜)
不规则的变化形式	man-men, woman-women, foot-feet(英尺), tooth-teeth, mouse-mice（老鼠），child-children
复合名词的复数形式	将后一部分变为复数 Englishman—Englishmen, gentleman—gentlemen, policeman—policemen, grown-up—grown-ups(成年人) 将主要成分变成复数 looker-on —lookers-on(旁观者)，passer-by — passers-by（路人） 将两部分都变成复数，前一词必须是 man 或 woman men doctors (男医生)， men drivers (男司机)， women singers(女歌手)，women teachers (女教师)

☞ 思考：German 的复数形式是什么？

● 不可数名词

什么叫不可数名词(uncountable nouns)？有哪些种类的不可数名词？

不可数名词是不能用数目计算的事物的名词。这类词不能在前面加 a/an 或在后面加 s 变成复数。

不可数名词的种类

表示物质或材料的	beer, blood, coffee, juice, oil, wine, paper, bread, butter, cheese, ice, meat, beef, chicken, chalk, copper, gold, silver, iron, steel, water, cotton, air, oxygen, fog, smoke
表示动作、性质、状态、情感等抽象概念的	birth, happiness, evolution, technology（科技）, management(管理)
表示无生命的集合名词	furniture, machinery（机械）, equipment, jewelry, traffic, clothing, luggage (行李)

☞ 思考：不可数名词的数量是如何表示的？

● 主谓一致

I *am* reading a legend story.
我正在读一本传奇小说。
He *is* reading a legend story.
他正在读一本传奇小说。
You *are* reading a legend story.
你在读一本传奇小说。
They *are* reading a legend story.
他们正在读一本传奇小说。
Mary *is* also reading a legend story.
玛丽也在读一本传奇小说。
All the students *like* the teacher.
所有的学生都喜欢这位老师。
The boy *likes* his teacher.
这个男孩喜欢他的老师。

谓语动词必须和主语在人称和数上保持一致，就是主语和谓语的一致。

简单地说就是主语是单数时谓语动词就用单数形式；主语是复数时谓语动词就用复数形式。

动词+-s = 单数　　名词+-s = 复数
I / You + 谓语动词复数

I *speak* Chinese.
我说汉语。
She *speaks* English.
她说英语。
You *are* a girl / boy.
你是一个女生 / 男生。
It *is* sunny.
今天阳光明媚。

※ 注：

1. 集合名词作主语时，如果表示整体概念，谓语动词用单数形式；如果表示其中的单个成员则谓语动词用复数形式。这类名词常见的有：**family, party, committee, army, audience, class, city, company, nation, university** 等。

{ The family *lives* in a large house. 这一家住在一幢大房子里。
{ The family *love* singing. 这家人爱唱歌。

{ The city *is* beautiful. 这个城市很美。
{ The city *are* hospitality. 这个城市的人很热情。

2. **none of + n. / pron.** 作主语时，谓语既可以用复数也可以用单数。

{ None of them *is* mine. (✓)
{ None of them *are* mine. (✓)
这些东西都不是我的。

{ None of my sisters *is* interested in the music. (✓)
{ None of my sisters *are* interested in the music. (✓)
我的姐妹们都对音乐不感兴趣。

3. 由 **either...or...** 或者 **neither...nor, not only...but also...** 来连接两个并列主语时，采用就近原则——谓语动词在人称和数上跟最后一个名词或代词保持一致。

{ Either you or he *is* wrong.
{ Either he or you *are* wrong.
你和他有一个人错了。

{ Neither you nor he *is* wrong.
{ Neither he nor you *are* wrong.
既不是他错也不是你错。

{ Not only we but also he *is* going to the movies.
{ Not only he but also we *are* going to the movies.
我们和他都要去看电影。

 ## 重点及难点 (Key points)

● 特殊名词

有很多的名词既可作可数名词又可作不可数名词，而且词义会发生变化。

单数	复数
time 时间	times 次数
cloth 布	clothes 衣服
work 工作	works 工厂，著作
paper 纸	papers 试卷、论文、报纸
glass 玻璃	glasses 玻璃杯、眼镜
room 空间、余地	rooms 房间
wood 木头	woods 森林
facility 方便、便利	facilities 设备、装备
sand 沙子	sands 沙滩

● 谓语动词用单数的情况

1. 不定式、动名词短语或者名词性从句作主语时，谓语动词用单数。

To become actresses *is* their ambition.
做演员是她们的雄心。
Nodding often *means* you say "yes."
点头经常意味着你表示同意。
What I want to know *is* who is he.
我想知道的就是他是谁。

2. 事件、国名、机构名称、作品名称用作主语时，谓语动词用单数。

The United States *is* a country with advanced science and technology.
美国是一个科学技术发达的国家。
The United Nations *was* formed in 1945.
联合国成立于 1945 年。

The Thirty-Nine Steps is an interesting novel.
《三十九级台阶》是一本很有意思的小说。

3. > 表示度量、距离、金额、时间等名词复数作主语时，谓语动词用单数形式。

Fifteen years *represents* a long period of his life.
15年代表他一生中一个很长的时期。
One hundred miles *is* too far to travel on foot.
100英里太远了，徒步很难走到。
Ten thousand dollars *is* a large sum of money.
10000美元是一大笔钱。

4. > 单数词作主语，虽然后接由 including, as well as, together with, in addition to, accompanied by 等词连接的其他词，谓语动词仍用单数。

Gold, as well as silver, *has* recently risen in price.
最近金银的价格涨了。
The factory, with all its equipment, *has* been burned.
这家工厂连同设备一起被烧了。

5. > a portion of, a series of, a kind of 等词语修饰主语时，谓语动词用单数。

A series of pre-recorded tapes *has* been prepared for language laboratory use.
已准备好一系列预先录制的磁带供语言试验室使用。

6. > 用不定代词 each, every, no, either, neither, another, the other 等修饰的主语，以及用 something, anything, nothing, everything, somebody, someone, anybody, anyone, nobody, everybody, everyone 作主语时，谓语动词用单数形式。

No one *agrees* with him.
没有人同意他的意见。
Every person *has* seen that.
每个人都看到了。
Either of them *is* OK.
他们两个哪一个都行。

Someone *wants* to see you.
有人找你。

● 谓语动词用复数的情况

1. both, some, few, many, several 等词语用作主语或修饰主语时,谓语动词用复数。

Both of them *have* gone to Shanghai on business.
他们两个人都去上海出差了。
Few of my classmates really *understand* me.
我的同学中没几个真正理解我。
Several students *were* late for school yesterday.
昨天几个同学上课迟到了。

2. 形容词前加定冠词泛指时,谓语动词用复数。

In many western films, **the good** *are* well rewarded and **the bad** *are* punished.
在很多西方电影中,好人有好报、恶人有恶报。

应用 (Practice)

I. Choose the correct answer. (选择正确的答案)

1. In his speech, he gave us _____ on how to learn English.
   A. some advice   B. some advices
   C. several advices   D. an advice

2. I'd like _____ about the management of your hotel, please.
   A. some informations   B. some information
   C. an information   D. many informations

3. Those _____ wanted to buy some _____.
   A. women doctors, teeth-brushes   B. woman doctors, tooth-brush
   C. women doctor, teeth-brushes   D. women doctors, tooth-brushes

4. _____ been made in science since then.
   A. A great progress has   B. Great progresses have
   C. Great progress has   D. Many progresses have

87

5. He dropped the _____ and broke it.
   A. cup of coffee   B. coffee's cup
   C. cup for coffee   D. coffee cup
6. A _____ of money has been spent on the building.
   A. great deal   B. good many
   C. plenty   D. great number
7. China has _____ of more than 1.2 billion.
   A. much population   B. many population
   C. a little population   D. a large population
8. "Why couldn't they meet us at five o'clock?"
   "Because they were delayed by _____."
   A. a heavy traffic   B. heavy traffic
   C. some heavy traffics   D. traffic being heaby
9. He invited all his _____ to join in his wedding party.
   A. comrades-ins-arms   B. comrades-in-arm
   C. comrade-in-arms   D. comrade-in-arms
10. All the _____ in the hospital will get a rise tomorrow.
    A. women-doctors   B. woman doctors
    C. women doctors   D. doctors of women
11. How happy they are! They are _____.
    A. in high spirits   B. in high spirit
    C. in a high spirit   D. in the high spirit
12. The fire started in the basement and quickly spread to the first floor, where it destroyed all the _____ in the language lab.
    A. furnitures and equipments   B. furniture and equipment
    C. furniture and equipments   D. furnitures and equipment
13. We are going to have _____ quiz.
    A. a few minutes   B. a few minute
    C. a few minutes'   D. a few minutes's

II. **Tick the correct form of the verb in brackets in each of the following sentences.** (在下列句子中选择合适的动词)

1. Every one of my brothers (has, have) brown eyes.
2. Here (is, are) the documents you asked for.
3. Some of the money (is, are) missing.
4. Half of the students in the class (is, are) from the North.
5. Two thousand miles (is, are) too far for us to travel over a short vacation.
6. One hundred and sixty pounds (is, are) what you should weigh.
7. Jane is one of the people who (is, are) willing to help others.
8. You are the one who (is, are) wrong.

Unit 9 名词的数和主谓一致

9. All of the work (has, have) been finished.
10. Neither the teacher nor the students (has, have) enough time.
11. The team (is, are) trying on the new boots.
12. A number of students (speaks, speak) English well.
13. My friend and classmate Paul (race, races) motorcycles in his spare time.
14. Few members of the party (approves, approve) the commettee's appointment.
15. The Daily News (says, say) it's going to rain.
16. One or perhaps more pages (is, are) missing.
17. The windows of the shop (is, are) anything but clean.
18. The smallest of the boys (is, are) the cleverest in class.
19. Neither she nor they (is, are) ready to go home.
20. Neither of the chairs (is, are) very comfortable.
21. The mob (is, are) picking up whatever they could lay hands on.
22. How much (is, are) those books?
23. The audience (is, are) usually small.
24. All but him and me (is, are) going to the cinema.
25. A series of accidents (has, have) occurred in Queensway.

Unit 10　动词的种类 (Kinds of Verbs)

导入 (Lead-in)

☞ 思考：动词表示的一定是动作吗？动词在句中起什么作用呢？

看下面两段文字，注意斜体部分的词，想想它们是什么意思，并观察它们在句中所起的作用。

　　Different cultures *have* very different attitudes to time. People from Northern European backgrounds *tend* to be very strict about adhering to time. An appointment at 11a.m. *will see* a German or a British person *arrive* at or before that time. However, a Spanish or Italian person *may feel* that being 10 or 15 minutes late *is* not really a problem.

　　Socializing is usually separate from business in some cultures. The office *is* the office—and activities outside work *have* nothing to do with business relationships. In other cultures, almost all important business decisions *may* be taken within a social context—at meals or other informal activities.

讲解 (Explanation)

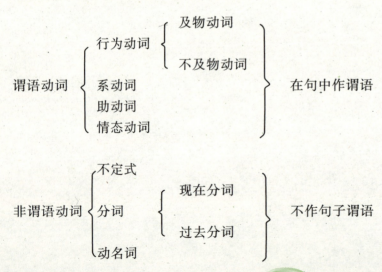

Unit 10　动词的种类

● 行为动词

I really **enjoy** chatting with friends on line.
我很喜欢在网上和朋友聊天。
I **spent** all my spare time surfing the internet.
我把所有的业余时间都用来上网。
Whether he will come doesn't **matter.**
他来不来没关系。
The museum **opens** at 10 in the morning.
博物馆早上10点开门。

> 比较前两句中的动词和后两句中的动词，体会及物和不及物动词的区别。

> 及物动词(vt.)指后面能接宾语的动词；不及物动词(vi.)指后面不直接接宾语的动词。

☞ 思考：有没有动词既能作及物动词，又可作不及物动词呢？

● 系动词

The leaves **turned** red.
树叶变红了。
I am **confused** when I come across some abbreviations.
遇到一些缩写形式时我总是弄不明白。
It **seems** ages since we heard from you.
好久没有你的消息了。

> 你知道还有其他哪些常见的系动词吗？系动词后常接什么结构？

> 系动词后接表语，说明主语的性质、特征和状态等。能作表语的有名词、形容词、副词、不定式、介词结构、分词、从句等。常见的系动词有：be, seem, appear, feel, look, sound, taste, keep, turn, become, get, stay, remain 等。

● 助动词

They **are** discussing their plans.
他们在讨论他们的计划。

> 什么时候该用助动词？常见的助动词有哪些？

Do you want me to bring something to drink?
要我带点什么喝的来吗？

You **are** not required to stay.
没有要求你留下来。

The World Wide Web **has** become a powerful medium for sharing information.
万维网已经成为一种分享信息的强大媒体。

He **will** be back in a few minutes.
他一会儿就回来。

> 助动词主要有：be, do, have, will / shall。助动词的作用是与行为动词或系动词一起构成一定的时态（进行时、完成时、将来时）、语态（被动），以及疑问句和否定句。

☞ 思考：助动词 be 和系动词 be 一样吗？

● 情态动词

It **would** be nice if you could come.
如果你能来的话就太好了。

We **should** try and do something together soon.
我们应该找时间聚一聚。

If an invitation **must** be refused, most people expect a reason.
如果的确需要回绝邀请，多数邀请人希望得到解释。

Could you give me your name and telephone number, please?
能告诉我你的名字和电话号码吗？

情态动词	表示
can, could	能力；可能性；请求，许可
may, might	可能性；许可
will, would, shall (仅用于第一人称)	意愿；征求对方意见
should, ought to	应该(劝告或责任)；推测或可能
must, have to	必须；推测
need	需要，有必要性
dare	敢于做某事

> could, would, might 是 can, will, may 的过去式；当它们不用于过去时态中时，表达的语气相对于 can, will, may 更加委婉。

重点及难点(Key points)

● 动词短语

动词短语(verb phrases)是动词的一种固定搭配形式,在句中很常见。以下是动词短语搭配的五种基本类型:

1. 动词+副词

Please **turn on** the light. (**turn the light on, turn it on**).
请打开灯。
Something unexpected has **turned up**.
意外情况出现了。

2. 动词+介词

I'm **looking for** my watch.
我在找我的手表。

3. 动词+副词+介词

Let's hurry and **catch up** with them.
咱们快点儿吧,赶上他们。

4. 动词+名词

Shall we **take a rest**?
我们休息一下,好吗?

5. 动词+名词+介词

Who will **take care of** the baby?
谁来照顾孩子?

 应用 (Practice)

I. Read the following dialogue. Find out the verbs or the verb phrases and tell what kinds of verbs do they belong. (读下面的对话,找出动词或动词短语,并说说它们分别属于哪种动词。)

Customer: I'd like to check in, please.
Clerk: Certainly. Do you have a reservation?
Customer: Yes. The name is Morales.
Clerk: Here we are. May I take a look at your passport, please?

Customer: OK, here you are.
Clerk: Thank you. Could you fill in the registration card, please? And I'll need your credit card.
Customer: All right.
Clerk: Thank you. And here's your room key. Room 321.
Customer: Does the room have an ocean view?
Clerk: No. Rooms with an ocean view are $15 more per night. Your room overlooks... the parking lot.
Customer: Well, I'd like a room with an ocean view, please.
Clerk: I'm sorry. Those rooms are all taken.

II. **Fill in the blanks with the proper words given below, making necessary changes.** (选词,并用其适当形式填空。)

> turn   get   become   grow   look   taste   keep   seem

1. She _____ silent all night.
2. It rained a lot, and the crops _____ fast.
3. She _____ young for her age.
4. The questions _____ easy at first, but later I found them very difficult.
5. The moon cake _____ good.
6. My brother _____ a teacher last year.
7. Hearing the bad news, her face _____ pale.
8. It _____ dark. Let's go home

III. **Which one has the same meaning as the sentence given, A or B?** (A 和 B 中哪一个句子与所给的句子意思相同？)

1. It's impossible that it is true.
   A. It mightn't be true.　　　　　B. It can't be true.
2. It could be that they are not married.
   A. They may not be married.　　B. They can't be married.
3. It is necessary that I be home before 11 o'clock.
   A. I should be home before 11.　B. I must be home before 11.
4. You want to know whether I want to join you.
   A. Would you like to join us?　　B. Could you join us?
5. You want to use my phone, and you want to be particularly polite.
   A. Could I use your phone?　　 B. Can I use your phone?
6. You want to leave your books with me.
   A. Can't you leave your books with me?　B. Can I leave my books with you?

Unit 11 动词的时态 (Tenses)

导入 (Lead-in)

☞ 思考：汉语是怎么表示事情发生的时间的？

> 读读下面这个小故事，想想它讲的是过去、现在还是将来的事。你是根据什么判断的？

　　Before lunch, Brian happened to see a man in rags fishing in a ditch about five meters outside a bar. All people passing by the man looked at him as if he were a foolish man.
　　Brian's heart went out of him. He said kindly to the man, "Hello, will you please do me a favor and have a drink with me in the bar?"
　　The man gladly accepted the invitation. After buying the man several soft drinks, Brian asked, "You're fishing, aren't you? May I ask how many fishes you caught this morning?"
　　"You are the eighth," said the man, with a smile.

讲解 (Explanation)

一般时态

> 一般时态(Simple Tenses)包括哪些时态？它们分别表示什么？

The Gateway Arch **is** the tallest man-made monument in the Western Hemisphere.
大拱门是西半球最高的人工纪念碑。
He **likes** steak, but he **doesn't like** chicken.
他喜欢牛排，但不喜欢鸡肉。
A man **offered** me a job during my trip to Australia.
在澳大利亚旅行时有人给我提供了一份工作。
He **lived** in Brazil for two years.
他在巴西住了两年。
He **will** arrive tomorrow morning.
他明天上午到。

I'**m going to meet** him at the airport.
我要去机场接他。
The lecture **is to begin** at two in the afternoon.
讲座下午两点开始。

	动词形式	标志
一般现在时	do/does	often, usually, always, sometimes, rarely, seldom, never, every (day/month), (once/twice) a week ...
一般过去时	did	just now, used to, yesterday, last (week/year), (three years) ago, (two days) before, in (1990),...
一般将来时	will do is/am/are going to do is/am/are to do is/am/are about to do (即将发生)	in the future, tomorrow, next (week/month/year)...

(do 表示动词原形，does 表示动词的第三人称单数形式，did 表示动词过去时。)

> 一般现在时表示经常或反复发生的动作、存在的状态，主语的特征、性格、能力，或客观事实或普遍真理；
> 一般过去时表示过去某一时间发生的动作或存在的状态；
> 一般将来时表示的是将来要发生的动作或情况。

☞ 思考：一般现在时在某些情况下可以表示将来吗？

● 进行时态

> 进行时态 (Continuous Tenses) 包括哪些时态？它们有什么共同特点？

He **is learning** English now.
现在他在学英语。
Aren't you **teaching** at the university now?
你不是在大学教书吗？
I **was watching** TV when she called.
她打电话的时候，我正在看电视。
Yesterday at this time, I **was sitting** at my desk at work.
昨天这个时候，我正坐在桌旁工作。
He **will be studying** at the library tonight.
他今晚会在图书馆学习。
Are you **going to be waiting** for her when her plane arrives tonight?
今晚她的飞机到的时候，你会等她吗？

	动词形式
现在进行时	is/am/are doing
过去进行时	was/were doing
将来进行时	will be doing; is/am/are going to do

（do 表示动词原形，doing 表示动词的现在分词。）

> 现在 / 过去 / 将来进行时表示现在 / 过去 / 将来某一时刻或某一时间段正在进行的动作或发生的事情。

☞ 思考：所有的动词都有进行时吗？

● 完成时

> 完成时态(Perfect Tenses)包括哪些时态？相应的动词形式是什么？

Nobody **has** ever **climbed** that mountain.
没人爬过那座山。
My English **ha**s really **improved** since I moved to Australia.
自从我移居澳大利亚之后，我的英语水平有了很大提高。
Doctors **have cured** many deadly diseases.
医生们治愈了许多致命的疾病。
She **had** never **been** to an opera before last night.
昨晚之前，她从未去看过歌剧。
I didn't have any money because I **had lost** my wallet.
那时我没钱，因为我丢了钱包。
By next November, I **will have received** my promotion.
到明年十一月前，我会得到提升。
How many countries **are** you **going to have visited** by the time you turn 50?
50 岁的时候，你去过的国家会有多少？

	动词形式	标志
现在完成时	have/has done	yet, since..., so far, up to now, this week, this month, in the last year, ...
过去完成时	had done	before + (past time), before...did
将来完成时	will have done is/am/are going to have done	by+(future time)

（did 表示动词过去式，done 表示动词的过去分词。）

> 现在完成时表示在现在以前某一不确定的时间，事情发生了。常表示经验、改变或成就；
> 过去完成时表示在过去某一具体时间或某事之前，事情发生了。
> 将来完成时表示在将来某一具体时间或某事之前，事情要发生。

☞ 思考：有些动词的完成时形式不能跟表示一段时间的状语连用，是哪些动词呢？

● 完成进行时

She **has been working** at that company for three years.
三年来她一直在那家公司工作。
I **have been feeling** really tired recently.
最近我总觉得很累。
I **had been waiting** there for more than two hours when she finally arrived.
我等了两个多小时她才来。
Mike wanted to sit down because he **had been standing** all day at work.
迈克想坐下来，因为他已经站着工作一整天了。

	动词形式	标志
现在完成进行时	have/has been doing	for (two weeks), for (the last 30 minutes), since ..., recently, lately
过去完成进行时	had been doing	before...did when...did

(did 表示动词的过去式，doing 表示动词的现在分词。)

> 现在完成进行时表示开始于过去，并持续到现在的动作或事情。
> 过去完成进行时表示开始于过去，并持续到过去的某个时间的动作或事情。

☞ 思考：完成进行时(Perfect Continuous Tenses)和完成时最大的区别是什么？

重点及难点 (Key points)

● 非延续性动词

非延续性动词也叫瞬间动词,表示动作很快结束,不能持续。
如:go, come, arrive, leave, die, buy, open, close, begin, finish, borrow, lend, see...

> 非延续性动词在肯定句中不能与表示一段时间的状语连用。

He has *left*.　　　　　　　　(√)　　I have *borrowed* the book　　　　　　　(√)
他走了。　　　　　　　　　　　　　　我借了这本书。
He has *left* **for an hour.**　(×)　　I have *borrowed* the book **for three months**　(×)
He has *been away* for an hour. (√)　I have *kept* the book for three months.　(√)
他走了一个小时了。　　　　　　　　　这本书我借了三个月。

> 若要与表示一段时间的状语连用,非延续性动词须转换成延续性动词或短语。常见的转换有:
>
> leave—be away(from)　　　borrow—keep
> die—be dead　　　　　　　buy—have
> begin/start—be on　　　　finish—be over
> fall asleep—be asleep　　get up—be up
> come here—be here　　　go there—be there
> become—be　　　　　　　come back—be back
> get to/arrive—be(in/at)　return—be back

The concert **has been on** for half an hour.
音乐会已经开始半个小时了。
They **have** already **been back** for two weeks.
他们已经回来两个星期了。

> 非延续性动词的进行时形式不能表示动作正在进行,而是表示动作将要发生。

They **are arriving** tonight.
他们今晚到。
I'**m not going** to the party tonight.
我今晚不去参加聚会。

一般现在时和现在进行时表示将来

> 动词的一般现在时可以表示将要实行的计划或安排，尤指时刻安排。

The train **leaves** tonight at 6 PM.
火车下午6点离开。
When **do** we board the plane?
我们什么时候上飞机？
When **does** class begin tomorrow?
明天的课几点开始？

> 在时间、条件等从句中，不用将来时，而用一般现在时表示一般将来，用现在进行时表示将来进行，用现在完成时表示将来完成。

I will call you when I **arrive**.
我到了会给你打电话的。
I will stay at home if it **rains** tonight.
要是今晚下雨，我就呆在家里。
If I **am** elected, I will make sure everyone has access to inexpensive health insurance.
如果我当选，我保证每个人都能获得低廉的医疗保险。
I am going to play basketball when I **have finished** my homework.
做完作业后我要去打篮球。
While you **are studying** at home, Kate will be in class.
你在家学习的时候，凯蒂将会在上课。

> 动词的进行时形式可以表示事情即将发生或计划。延续性动词的进行时形式表示将来时，一般都有将来的时间状语。

I'**m meeting** some friends after work.
下班后我要见几个朋友。
He **is visiting** his parents this weekend.
他这周末要去看父母。

☞ 思考：怎么判断动词的进行时形式表示的动作是正在发生还是将要发生呢？

Unit 11 动词的时态

应用 (Practice)

I. **Read the following passage. Analyze the tenses used.**（阅读下面的一段文章，分析所用的时态。）

   I've got a cell phone, email and voice mail. But why am I so lonely?

   A funny thing happened on the way to the communications revolution: we stopped talking to one another.

   I was walking in the park with a friend recently, and his cell phone rang, interrupting our conversation. There they were, talking and talking on a beautifully sunny day and I became invisible, absent from the conversation.

   The telephone used to connect you to the absent. Now it makes people sitting next to you feel absent.

   Why is it that the more connected we get, the more disconnected I feel?

II. **Choose from the four choices the most appropriate one to complete the sentences.** （从四个选项中选择最合适的完成句子。）

1. Jim: Do you want to come over for dinner tonight?
   Denise: Oh, I'm sorry, I can't. I _____ to a movie tonight with some friends.
   A. go   B. have gone
   C. am going   D. went

2. I _____ a mystery movie on TV when the electricity went out.
   A. watch   B. am watching
   C. watched   D. was watching

3. You look really great! _____ out at the fitness center recently?
   A. Have you been working   B. Are you working
   C. Were you working   D. Did you work

4. If it _____ this weekend, we will go skiing near Lake Tahoe.
   A. snows   B. is snowing
   C. will snow   D. is going to snow

5. I _____ many pictures of the pyramids before I went to Egypt.
   A. see   B. saw
   C. have seen   D. had seen

6. I am sick of rain and bad weather! Hopefully, when we wake up tomorrow morning, the sun _____.
   A. will shine   B. will be shining
   C. will have shined D. shines

7. Jenny _____ for ten minutes. She is exercising over there.
   A. got up   B. has got up
   C. has been up   D. gets up

101

8. Right now, I _____ for my best friend who was here just now.
   A. look   B. am looking
   C. was looking   D. have looked

9. By the time I got to the office, the meeting _____ without me.
   A. began   B. has begun
   C. had begun   D. was beginning

10. I _____ chocolate since I was a child.
    A. love   B. had loved
    C. loved   D. have loved

III. Fill in the blanks with the proper forms of the words given. (用所给词的适当形式填空。)

1. Every Monday Mary (drive) _____ her kids to football practice.

2. A: I (call) _____ you last night after dinner, but you (be, not) _____ there. Where were you?
   B: I (work) _____ out at the fitness center.

3. I (have) _____ the same car for more than ten years. I (think) _____ about buying a new one.

4. It's strange that you (call) _____ because I (think, just) _____ about you.

5. When I return to Australia, I (study) _____ for nine months.

6. In the last hundred years, traveling (become) _____ much easier and very comfortable. In the 19th century, it (take) _____ two or three months to cross North America by covered wagon. The trip (be) _____ very rough and often dangerous. Things (change) _____ a great deal in the last hundred and fifty years. Now you can fly from New York to Los Angeles in a matter of hours.

7. I (not travel) _____ much yet; however, I (visit) _____ the Grand Canyon and San Francisco by the time I leave the United States.

8. I am going on a dream vacation to Tahiti. While you (do) _____ paperwork and (talk) _____ to annoying customers on the phone, I (lie) _____ on a sunny, tropical beach.

9. When I (turn) _____ the radio on yesterday, I (hear) _____ a song that was popular when I was in high school. I (hear, not) _____ the song in years, and it (bring) _____ back some great memories.

10. Lately, I (think) _____ about changing my career because I (become) _____ dissatisfied with the conditions at my company.

Unit 12 动词的语态 (Voice)

导入 (Lead-in)

看看下面的句子，想想箭头方向的变化表示的是什么意思？

Mark bought *a car*.　　　　　　　　*A car* was bought by **Mark**.

I have damaged *your bicycle*.　　　*Your bicycle* has been damaged by **me**.

He is repairing *the pipe*.　　　　　*The pipe* is being repaired by **him**.

☞ 思考：主动语态和被动语态有何区别？英语中是主动语态用得多，还是被动语态用得多？什么情况下用被动语态比较好？

讲解 (Explanation)

主动语态 ⇒ 主语是动作发出者

被动语态 ⇒ 主语是动作承受者

● 被动语态的基本结构和时态

Sally **was invited** to a party.
沙莉受邀参加了一个聚会。

The windows **are cleaned** regularly.
窗户定期清洁。

It **was reported** that over 50 people **were killed** in the accident.
据报道，有 50 多人死于事故。

All the preparations **have been completed.**
所有的准备工作都完成了。
Letters **will be sent** to you directly.
信会直接寄给你。
The trees **had** already **been cut** down before they got there.
他们到那儿之前,树已经砍掉了。
The bridge **is being rebuilt** right now.
桥正在重修。

> 被动语态(passive voice)基本结构:be + 过去分词

	主动	被动
一般现在时	do	**is/am/are** done
一般过去时	did	**was/were** done
一般将来时	will do, is/am/are going to do	will **be** done is/am/are going to **be** done
现在进行时	is/am/are doing	is/am/are **being** done
过去进行时	was/were doing	was/were **being** done
现在完成时	have/has done	have/has **been** done
过去完成时	had done	had **been** done
将来完成时	will have done	will have **been** done

(do 表示动词原形,did 表示动词过去式,doing 表示动词现在分词,done 表示动词过去分词)

> 被动语态(be + 过去分词)的时态由 be 来体现,过去分词不变。

☞ 思考:是不是所有的动词都有被动语态?

● **被动语态的适用情况**

> 主动和被动句,哪个表达的意思更清楚?

Sally was invited to the party.
沙莉应邀参加聚会。
Jane invited Sally to the party.
简邀请沙莉参加聚会。

I was distracted.
我分心了。
The tax problem distracted me.
税务问题让我分心了。

> 因为被动语态可以不指出动作发出者，所以相比较而言，被动语态有时会显得表意不清。因此一般情况下应用主动语态。

适合用被动语态的情况如下：

> 强调动作承受者

A mistake was made.（强调 a mistake，比较礼貌、客气。）
You made a mistake.（强调 you）

> 动作发出者未知。

My wallet was stolen.
我的钱包被偷了。（不知道是谁偷的。）
Over 100 different contaminants have been dumped into the river.
100 多种污染物被倒进了河里。（不知道是谁倒的。）

> 动作发出者是谁不重要，或人所共知。

The parcel will be delivered to your house tomorrow.
包裹会在明天送到你的家。

☞ 思考：为什么在有些说明性或科学性较强的文章中被动语态用得比较多？

● **被动语态的特殊结构**

He **got arrested** soon after that.
之后不久他就被逮捕了。
Fortunately, nobody **got hurt.**
幸运的是，没有人受伤。
Nothing **can be decided** right now.
现在，什么都还无法定下来。
The problem **may not be solved** easily.
问题可能不会那么容易解决。

> "get + 过去分词"也可表示被动。
> 带情态动词的被动结构为：情态动词 + be + 过去分词。

非谓语动词的被动语态

He doesn't like **being told** what to do.
他不喜欢别人告诉他该去做什么。

She is very excited about **being invited**.
获得了邀请，她很兴奋。

Having been taught three times, she still didn't know how to do it.
教了她三次了，她还是不知道怎么做。

They waited there **to be chosen**.
他们等着被挑选.

I want **to be given** a special assignment.
我想得到一个特别的任务。

> doing 的被动语态是 being done
> to do 的被动语态是 to be done

重点及难点 (Key points)

主动语态和被动语态的互换

句子变化语态时的特殊情况：

> 主动语态中谓语有双宾语，变成被动语态时用一个宾语作主语，另一个留在谓语后面。

His father gave **him a birthday present**.→
他父亲给了他一个生日礼物。
{ **A birthday present** was given to him by his father.
He was given a birthday present by his father.

> 主动语态中有宾语补足语时，变成被动语态时宾补留在谓语后面，不作变动。

Someone saw the boy **smoking a cigarette**.→
有人看见这个男孩抽烟。
The boy was seen **smoking a cigarette**.

People found him **dead in his room**.→
人们发现他在房间里死去了。
He was found **dead in his room**.

> 作谓语的动词短语是一个整体,不可随意删减.

They **are taking good care of** the children.→
他们把孩子照顾得很好。
The children **are being taken good care of** by them.

She **has turned** the light on.→
她把灯开了。
The light **has been turned on** by her.

> 主动语态 make sb. do,变成被动语态时要加上 to,即 sb. be made to do。

They made us **stay** in the building.→
他们让我们呆在楼里。
We were made **to stay** in the building.

● 主动形式表示被动

> break,catch,clean,drive,lock,open,sell,read,write,wash 等动词,当它们被用作不及物动词来描述主语特征时,常用其主动形式 表达被动意义,主语通常是物。

These shirts **wash** easily.
这些衬衫容易洗。
The book she wrote doesn't **sell** very well.
她写的那本书卖得不太好。

> 在 need,want,require,bear,worth 等词的后面,动名词用主动形式表示被动意义。

The car **needs washing**.
车需要洗洗了。
The novel is **worth reading**.
这本书值得一读。

应用 (Practice)

I. **Read the following passage, and find out passive sentences.** （阅读下面的一段文章，找出被动句。）

The students may take coursework at another institution of higher education. For all courses other than general studies, the student must obtain prior written permission from the dean of the college in which the student is enrolled; for general study courses, prior written permission must be obtained from the dean of the University College. These course will be listed on the official academic record（成绩报告单）. Each course will reflect the course number, title, grade-point and credit value; no grade-point value will appear on the record and no grade-point average will be calculated for the coursework listed.

II. **Choose from the four choices the most appropriate one to complete the sentence.** （从四个选项中选择最合适的完成句子。）

1. Great changes have taken place in the city, and a lot of factories _____.
   A. set up   B. have set up   C. have been set up   D. were setting up

2. The coat _____ over 100 dollars.
   A. cost   B. is cost   C. is costing   D. has been cost

3. This page needs _____.
   A. to check
   C. being checked
   B. checking
   D. checked

4. The books on the table _____ Professor Atwood.
   A. belongs
   C. belongs to
   B. are belonged to
   D. belong to

5. Rainforests _____ and burned at such a speed that they will disappear from the earth in the near future.
   A. cut   B. are cut   C. are being cut   D. are cutting

6. — _____ the sports meet might be put off.
   —Yes, it all depends on the weather.
   A. I've been told
   C. I'm told
   B. I've told
   D. I told

7. —What do you think of the book?
   —Oh, excellent. It's worth _____ a second time.
   A. to read   B. to be read   C. reading   D. being read

8. I need one more stamp before my collection _____.
   A. has completed
   C. has been completed
   B. completes
   D. is completed

9. Don't drop the ink on your shirt, for it _____ easily.
   A. won't wash out   B. won't be washed out
   C. isn't washed out   D. washes out
10. If city noises _____ from increasing, people _____ shout to be heard even at dinner.
   A. are not kept; will have to   B. are not kept; have
   C. do not keep; will have to   D. do not keep; have to
11. Having a trip is certainly good for them, but it remains _____ whether they will enjoy it.
   A. to see   B. to be seen
   C. seeing   D. seen
12. While shopping, people sometimes can't help _____ into buying something they don't really need.
   A. to persuaded   B. persuading
   C. being persuaded   D. be persuaded
13. —Have you moved into the new office?
    —Not yet, the rooms _____.
   A. have not painted   B. are painting
   C. are painted   D. are being painted
14. Who to invite to the party _____ yet.
   A. is not deciding   B. has not been decided
   C. is not being decided   D. has not decided
15. The boss entered the office and was happy to learn that almost all the seats _____.
   A. was booked   B. had been booked
   C. were booked   D. have been booked

III. Change the voice of the following sentences.（改变下列句子的语态。）

1. They sent us a letter the day before yesterday.
2. The dishes have not been washed by my little brother.
3. Will they invite him to the party?
4. They have closed the highway because of the snow.
5. Lots of houses were destroyed by the earthquake.
6. People speak German in Austria.
7. You must complete the report by next Friday.
8. We will not accept credit cards.
9. The waiter has not brought us the coffee.
10. The nurse is looking after the patient.

Unit 13　虚拟语气 (Subjunctive Mood)

导入 (Lead-in)

☞ 思考：汉语是怎么表示事情发生的时间的？

> 比较每组的三个句子，看它们的语气各有什么不同。

Mary opens the window.
Mary, open the window.
I request that Mary open the window.

Does Jim come here?
Jim, come here, please.
If Jim knew it, he would come here.

☞ 思考：英语有几种语气？是哪几种？

讲解 (Explanation)

> 英语语气包括：陈述语气、祈使语气、虚拟语气。

陈述语气：陈述事实。
祈使语气：表达请求和命令。
虚拟语气：表达与事实相反的假设，或愿望、建议、要求等。

> 虚拟语气在结构上有别于其他语气之处在于，动词的变化形式和其他语气不一样。

Unit 13　虚拟语气

● **非真实条件句**

> 非真实条件指的是什么？非真实条件句中动词的形式跟真实条件句有什么不一样？

If the place **weren't** so big, it *wouldn't be* so fun.
如果这地方没这么大，就不会这么好玩了。

He **would go** alone if he *knew* the mountains. He doesn't, so he needs a guide.
如果他了解这些山，他就自己去了。但他不了解，所以他需要一个向导。

If you **were** really great and powerful, you *would keep* your promises.
如果你真的有权有能力的话，你会遵守诺言的。

If she **had worked** harder, she *would have passed* the exam.
如果她学习更努力一些，她就通过考试了。

If we **hadn't had** that problem with the car, we *wouldn't have missed* the speech.
如果我们的车没出问题，我们就不会错过演讲了。

I'm busy next week. If I **had** time, I *would come* to your party.
我下周很忙。如果我有时间，我会参加你的聚会的。

If I **were** not visiting my grandmother tomorrow, I *would help* you study.
如果我明天不去看祖母，我会辅导你学习的。

If he **were** to leave tomorrow, we *could give* him a ride.
如果他明天走的话，他可以搭我们的车。

> 非真实条件句表达的是与事实相反的假设，从句和主句动词形式的变化因时态的不同而有所不同。

	从句（动词形式）	主句（动词形式）
与现在事实相反	did	would/could/should/might + do
与过去事实相反	had done	would/could/should/might + have done
与将来事实相反	did/were doing/were to do/ should do	would/could/should/might + do

(do 表示动词原形，did 表示动词过去式，done 表示动词过去分词)

> 非真实条件句中，用 **were** 取代 **was**。

☞ 思考：非真实条件句中，从句和主句表示的时间必须一致吗？

其他从句中的虚拟语气

> 在其他从句中虚拟语气也是通过动词来表现的。动词的变化形式主要有两种：时态前移和原形。

> 看看有哪些句型需要用虚拟语气？动词是怎么变化的？

If only she **were** here, then she *would speak* up.
如果她在这儿就好了，她会仗义执言的。

If only I **had passed** the exam.
要是我通过了考试就好了。

Don't look at me as if I **were** crazy!
不要那样看着我，就像我疯了一样。

He acted as though nothing **had happened.**
他装着什么都没有发生的样子。

He wishes he **had** a hammer.
他希望自己有一个榔头。

I wish it **were** summer.
我希望现在是夏天。

What if I **granted** you a kingdom?
要是我授予你一个王国，会怎么样呢？

What if somebody **were** to blow up that bridge?
如果有人要把那座桥炸毁，会怎么样呢？

I would rather you **came** next weekend.
我宁可你下周末来。

I'd rather you **had not done** that.
我真希望你没做那件事。

It is time that children **went** to bed.
到孩子们上床睡觉的时候了。

It is about time that you **studied** hard.
是你该好好学习的时候了。

> 在 **if only, wish, what if, as if (as though), would rather, it is time** 后的从句用虚拟语气，动词需把时态前移，表示现在用过去时，表示过去用过去完成时。

☞ 思考：what if, as if (as though), would rather 后只能用虚拟语气吗？

I suggest that you **(should) run**.
我建议你快跑。
I insist you **return** my things to me at once.
我坚决要求你马上把我的东西还给我。
They recommend he **remain** in jail for another six months
他们建议他应在监狱里再呆六个月。
He urged that the matter **be resolved** in a family court.
他极力主张这件事在家庭法院解决。
However, for your safety, we do require that you **(should) keep** your seat belt fastened at all times while seated.
不过，为了您的安全，我们要求您坐着的时候系好安全带。

> 看看这些句子有什么特点？动词是什么形式？

> 动词表示建议、要求、命令、愿望等的时候，宾语从句用虚拟语气，动词用(should+)原形，should 可省略。

It's desired that we **(should) get** everything ready by tonight.
希望我们在今晚前准备好。
It is extremely urgent that we **talk** with you right now, sir.
先生，我们必须马上和您谈谈。
It's essential that my kids **pitch** in.
我的孩子们有必要也出力。
It was very critical that everything **be done** on time.
关键是每件事都要按时做完。
It is imperative that we **keep** this confidential.
这件事我们千万要保密。
That's why it is important that this **be done** today.
那就是为什么今天要做完这件事的原因。

> 主句的形容词有什么特点？

> 在 **It is/was desired (suggested, demanded...)** 结构，以及 **It is/was important (necessary, essential, critical, vital, urgent...)** 结构中，后面的主语从句用虚拟，动词用(should+)原形，should 可省略。

My advice is that he **exercise** every day.
我的建议是他每天锻炼。
His requirement is that everyone **(should) be** computer literate.
他的要求是每个人都懂电脑。
My suggestion is that wind power **be** a major thrust for future electrical power generation.
我的建议是风力是未来发电的主要推动力。

> 句中从句所修饰的名词有什么特点？

The order came that everyone (**should**) **evacuate** from the building.
要求每个人从这栋楼撤退的命令下达了。

They rejected my proposal that we (**should**) **take** pollution into consideration.
他们拒绝了我要考虑环境污染的提议。

> 表示建议、要求、命令、愿望等的名词所带的同位语从句或表语从句，用虚拟语气，动词用(should+)原形，should 可省略。

 思考：上面三种句型中，从句都使用虚拟语气，主句在用词方面有什么共同之处吗？

重点及难点 (Key points)

● 时间错综的非真实条件句

> 非真实条件句中，主句和从句的时态不一定一致。如从句表示过去而主句表示现在，或从句表示现在而主句表示过去。

It *wouldn't be* so hot today if it **had rained** last night.
如果昨晚下雨了，今天就不会这么热了。

If I **were** a fascist, then I *would have sent* you to one of those Southern military academies a long time ago.
如果我是法西斯的话，我早把你送到南方的军事学院去了。

If we **hadn't been working** hard in the past few years, things *wouldn't be going* so smoothly.
如果我们在过去的几年里没有努力，现在的情况也不会这么顺利了。

If I **had invented** the personal computer, I *would be* rich now.
如果我发明了个人电脑，我现在就富了。

● 非真实条件句的倒装

> 非真实条件句可以倒装，目的是加强语气。倒装时省略 if，把 were, should 或 had 提到主语前。

Had Mark stayed in school, he *would have gotten* a better job.
如果马克那时呆在学校里，他找的工作会比现在的好。
Had he known that, he *would have decided* differently.
如果他之前知道的话，他会做出不同的决定的。
Should you be more careful, I *would be* happy.
你要是能更仔细些，我就高兴了。

● 非真实条件句的其他表现形式

> 有时候与事实相反的假设可以用介词结构，或上下文表现出来。

Without their help, our website *would not have been* possible.
要是没有他们的帮助，就不会有我们的网站。
Without your support, the company *would not be* a success.
要是没有你们的支持，公司现在不会成功的。
But for your help, we *would have lost* the game.
要是没有你们的支持，我们就输掉这场比赛了。
I *would not mind* you being so loud, but, you see, my baby is sleeping.
我本不介意你那么大声的，不过，我的孩子现在正在睡觉。

应用 (Practice)

I. **Read the following paragraphs. Point out the subjunctive mood.**（阅读下面的段落，指出虚拟语气。）

　　This would be wise advice, if only the situation were like that—if the job were done and it were time to relax. If only that were true! But challenges abound, and this is no time to take the future for granted.

　　If "the job" really were done, if there were nothing at stake except credit, perhaps it would be wiser to let the matter drop. But we are not in that position.

II. **Choose from the four choices the most appropriate one to complete the sentences.** （从四个选项中选择最合适的完成句子。）

　　1. The coach asked that each player ＿＿＿＿＿＿ twice each day.
　　　　A. practice　　　　　　　B. practices
　　　　C. practiced　　　　　　 D. would practice

115

2. We wished that we _____ New York's team.
   A. beat	B. were beaten
   C. had beaten	D. would have beaten

3. I would have grabbed the ball if I _____ closer to it.
   A. be	B. were
   C. was	D. had been

4. Team rules require that each player _____ responsible for memorizing one rule--and then for teaching that rule to all of the players.
   A. is	B. should be
   C. were	D. would be

5. Everything _____ if Albert hadn't called the police.
   A. should be destroyed	B. will have been destroyed
   C. would be destroyed	D. would have been destroyed

6. Supposing this ship _____, do you think there would be enough lifeboats for all the passengers?
   A. was sinking	B. sink
   C. were to sink	D. sank

7. Frankly, I'd rather you _____ anything for the time being.
   A. don't do	B. didn't do
   C. haven't done	D. won't do

8. It is about time we _____ something important to do.
   A. find	B. have found
   C. found	D. be finding

9. We required that the bags _____ paper.
   A. be made of	B. were made of
   C. would be made of	D. had been made of

10. The business is risky. But _____ we would be rich.
    A. if we succeed	B. would we succeed
    C. we should succeed	D. should we succeed

11. _____, we could not have finished the work on time.
    A. If they did not help us	B. Was it not for their help
    C. Should they offer to help us	D. But for their help

12. If only I _____ there.
    A. have not been	B. had not been
    C. not be	D. would not be

13. I would buy the car, but I _____ no money.
    A. had	B. have
    C. have had	D. had had

14. _____ to the doctor earlier, he might be alive today.
   A. If he went   B. Were he to go
   C. Should he go   D. Had he gone

15. I didn't go to the party last night, but I do wish that I _____ there.
   A. were   B. went
   C. was   D. had been

III. Fill in the blanks with the proper forms of the words given. (用所给词的适当形式填空。)

1. It is important that he (tell) _____ the truth now, lest he be doubted later.
2. I recommend that you (buy) _____ a second-hand pickup truck.
3. I wish he (be) _____ able to type faster.
4. I was going to request that television sets (turn down) _____.
5. If the kids (not eat) _____ all the ice cream, we would have had dessert.
6. I insisted that we (call) _____ for a police officer.
7. I wish it (be) _____ enough.
8. But if you were a scientist, I think you (ask) _____ yourself the same question.
9. He demanded that each driver (report) _____ his tips.
10. It is in the interest of the United States that Russia (be) _____ a democracy.

时态、语态及虚拟语气

I. In this section, there are 10 incomplete sentences. You are required to complete each one by deciding on the most appropriate word or words from the 4 choices marked A, B, C and D.

1. We didn't finish the work in time. You _____ us since your were there.
   A. might help   B. should help   C. could have helped   D. must have helped
2. It is required that anyone applying for a driver's license _____ a set of tests.
   A. take   B. takes   C. took   D. will take
3. The representative of the company demanded that part of the agreement _____ revised.
   A. will be   B. is   C. to be   D. be
4. It is most desirable that he _____ for the information by himself with a few clicks online.
   A. search   B. searched   C. has searched   D. will search
5. _____ he was seriously ill, I wouldn't have told him the truth.
   A. If I knew   B. If I know   C. Had I known   D. Did I know
6. This ATM has been out of service for a few days. It should _____ last week.
   A. fix   B. be fixed   C. have fixed   D. have been fixed
7. We could not have fulfilled the task in time if it _____ for their help.
   A. was not   B. is not   C. had not been   D. has not been
8. _____ last Friday, he would have got to Paris.
   A. Would he leave   B. Had he left
   C. If he is to leave   D. If he was leaving
9. I think it's high time we _____ strict measures to stop pollution.
   A. will take   B. take   C. took   D. have taken
10. The manager of the company insisted that all the staff members _____ the new safety rules.
    A. would observe   B. observe
    C. observed   D. will observe
11. I didn't go with them to the beach yesterday. But I do wish I _____ there.
    A. have been   B. had been   C. was   D. am
12. It is important that the committee _____ about the project at once.
    A. will be informed   B. be informed
    C. is informed   D. being informed

13. The committee members propose that the plan _____ postponed for a few days.
    A. to be   B. be   C. being   D. been
14. It's necessary that the problem _____ in some way or other.
    A. is settled   B. are settled   C. be settled   D. has been settled
15. It's high time we _____ something to stop road accidents.
    A. did   B. are doing   C. will do   D. do
16. I decide to leave the company next month, where I _____ for exactly three years.
    A. work   B. is working   C. will be working   D. will have worked
17. Every since I arrived here, I _____ in the dormitory because it is cheaper.
    A. lived   B. was living   C. had been living   D. have been living
18. He _____ in this company since he graduated from Andong Technical College ten years ago.
    A. worked   B. has been working
    C. had worded   D. was working
19. The car _____ by the side of the road and the driver tried to repair it.
    A. breaks down   B. was breaking down
    C. has broken down   D. broke down
20. Though he _____ well prepared before the job interview, he failed to answer some important questions.
    A. will be   B. would be   C. has been   D. had been
21. By the time you get to Shanghai tomorrow, I _____ for Chongqing.
    A. am leaving   B. will leave   C. shall have left   D. had left
22. This time next week I'll be on vacation. Probably I _____ on a beautiful beach.
    A. am lying   B. have lain   C. will be lying   D. will have lain
23. Linda feels exhausted because she _____ so many visitors today.
    A. has been having   B. had been having
    C. was having   D. had had
24. Most of the people who are visiting Britain _____ about the food and weather there.
    A. are always to complain   B. have always complained
    C. always complain   D. will always complain
25. The students _____ their papers by the end of this month.
    A. have finished   B. will be finishing
    C. will have finished   D. have been finishing
26. Since the introduction of the new techniques, the production cost _____ greatly.
    A. reduces   B. is reduced   C. is reducing   D. has been reduced
27. The project to clear up the polluted river _____ by the end of the next year.
    A. is being completed   B. has been completed
    C. will have been completed   D. will have completed
28. I hope they _____ this road by the time we come back next summer.
    A. have repaired B. are to repair   C. will repair   D. will have repaired

119

29. We won't be able to leave the office until the rain _____.
   A. will stop   B. stops   C. stopped   D. is stopping
30. Most of the machines in the workshop _____ next month.
   A. are repaired
   B. have been repaired
   C. were repaired
   D. will be repaired
31. By the time you get there tomorrow, they _____ for Beijing.
   A. will have left   B. are leaving   C. will leave   D. are to leave

II. There are 10 incomplete statements here. You should fill in each blank with the proper form of the word given in the brackets.

1. If we (know) _____ that the books were available, we would have bought them yesterday.
2. If he had taken his lawyer's advice, he (save) _____ himself a great deal of trouble.
3. The boy passed the final exams. But if he had spent more time on them, the results (be) _____ much better.
4. He might have been killed in that car accident yesterday if he (take) _____ part in that activity with the team.
5. It is important that he (be) _____ called back immediately.
6. He might not have been killed in the traffic accident yesterday if he (fasten) _____ the seat belt.
7. If I hadn't driven the car yesterday, I (avoid) _____ the accident.
8. Frankly speaking, I'd rather you (say) _____ nothing about it for the time being.
9. It is required that every employee (come) _____ in their uniform before 8:00 a.m
10. The director required that every member in his department (refer) _____ to this report.
11. If the team members had not helped me, I (fail) _____ in the last experiment.
12. I suggested that he (call) _____ on the director a week later.
13. The chairman required that every speaker (limit) _____ himself to fifteen minutes.
14. If I (not drink) _____ so much coffee yesterday afternoon, I would have been able to sleep well last night.
15. The boss insisted that Mr. Copper (give) _____ up his experiment at once.
16. Xiao Li speaks English in a way as if she (be) _____ an American.
17. If the medicine (take) _____ in time, it will be quite effective.
18. Tom took no notice of what I was saying because he thought I (cheat) _____ him.
19. By the end of next month, we (find) _____ a good solution to the technical problem.
20. John not only learnt Chinese but also (know) _____ the difference between his culture and ours.

21. By the end of this year the factory (produce) _____ 20,000 cell phones.
22. All the members of the club were present when the Chairman (elect) _____ last week.
23. As a rule, readers (not allow)_____ to take dictionaries out of the reading room.
24. By the end of last year, nearly a million cars (produce) _____ in that auto factory.
25. Before the flight takes off, all passengers (ask) _____ to fasten their seat belts.
26. We surely (find) _____ a good solution to the technical problems in the near future.
27. The villagers told us that a new bridge (build) _____ across the river in a year.
28. Jim told me he (join) _____ the army two years before.
29. Most students (take) _____ sixty credits by the time they graduate.
30. The cause of the accident may never (discover) _____ in spite of the effort of the police.
31. Jack must (go) _____ away —we can't find him anywhere in the factory.
32. He was told that the stranger (wait) _____ for him for 2 hours.
33. The police promised that they (try) _____ their best to look into the matter.
34. During the earthquake the room (shake) _____ and all the pictures fell off the wall.
35. We usually (go) _____ abroad for our holiday, but this year we are staying at home.
36. Hardly had we gathered in the square when it (begin) _____ to rain.
37. Nothing can (do) _____ unless we are given more information about the situation.
38. Sixty people (employ) _____ in this big factory last year.
39. As soon as I (get) _____ home, it started to rain heavily.
40. Up till now I (spend) _____ a great deal of money on books, magazines and newspapers.
41. In these five years, the foundation (collect) _____ a large amount of money.
42. The house with the furniture (buy) _____ for $50,000 last year.
43. On his way home he suddenly remembered that he (not lock) _____ the door of the office.
44. When I found Linda, she (play) _____ table tennis with her friend Jean.
45. The noise was so loud that it could (hear) _____ from far away.
46. The wine is in the fridge -it just wants (cool) _____ for a couple of minutes.
47. These pills should (keep) _____ out of the reach of the children.
48. In two hours' time he (finish) _____ his training and start work.

Unit 14 分词 (Participles)

导入 (Lead-in)

斜体部分的词跟动词有关系吗？如果有的话，是一种什么关系？

an *interesting* book, an *exciting* game
a *written* report, *developed* countries

看看下面的句子，想想斜体部分的词在句子中起什么作用。

I might be *interested* in that.
我可能会对它感兴趣。

It looks *interesting*.
看起来很有意思。

What's the *recommended* price?
建议价格是多少？

It's a game *based* on a TV programme.
这是根据一个电视节目设计出来的游戏。

The bus takes about 15 minutes, *depending* on the traffic.
坐公共汽车要花大约15分钟，这取决于交通状况。

I saw him *entering* the room.
我看见他进了房间。

Unit 14　分词

 讲解 (Explanation)

上面斜体部分的词都是分词。分词是动词的一种变化形式。

分词 ── 现在分词（动词 + ing，如 going, sitting）
　　　└ 过去分词（动词 + ed，如 invited, helped）

> 分词在句子中的作用与形容词或副词相当。

● **分词的功能**

Do you have a *preferred* **location**?
你有喜欢的地点吗？
But I didn't see him the *following* **day**.
但我第二天并没有见到他。
It is a **company** *specializing* in personnel recruitment.
这是一家专门从事人员招聘的公司。
The **question** *discussed* at the meeting is quite important.
会上讨论的问题很重要。
There is **nothing** *interesting*.
没有什么有趣的事。

> 分词在句中起什么作用？位置有什么特点？

> 分词在句中可以作定语。
> 单个分词作定语时一般放在被修饰词之前，但要放在 something, everything, anything, nothing 等不定代词之后；分词短语作定语也要放在被修饰词之后。

☞ 思考：分词短语作定语与定语从句有何关系？

Arriving at the destination, they were all exhausted.
当他们到达目的地时，都已筋疲力尽了。
Written in a hurry, this article was not so good.
因为写得匆忙，这篇文章不是很好。
Given an hour, I can work out the problem.
给我一个小时，我就能完成这道题。
He sat there silently, *moved* to tears.
他静静地坐在那里，感动得热泪盈眶。

> 分词短语在句中起什么作用？

123

Knowing what happened, he still made me pay for the damage.
尽管了解所发生的一切，他还是让我赔偿损失。
While *waiting* for the bus, we had a long talk.
等车的时候，我们聊了很长时间。

> **分词在句中可作状语。**
> 分词短语在句中可作时间、条件、原因、结果、让步、伴随等状语，其位置根据句意需要，可前可后。

☞ 思考：分词短语在句中作状语与副词从句有何关系？

The argument sounds *convincing*.
这个论点听起来很有说服力。
The film is quite *boring*.
那部电影挺无聊的。
They are *disappointed*.
他们很失望。
The dog became *alerted*.
那条狗警觉起来。

> **分词在句中可作表语。**
> 分词在句中作表语时，就相当于形容词。

We can **see** smoke *rising* from the chimneys.
我们能看到烟从烟囱里冒出来。
I **heard** an angel *singing*.
我听到天使在唱歌。
The most important thing is to **make** yourself *understood*.
最重要的是要让别人明白你的意思。
I want to **have** my car *washed* today.
我想今天把车洗了。

> 句中谓语动词有何特点？

> **分词在句中可作宾语补足语。**
> 分词在句中作宾补，其谓语动词一般为感官动词（see, hear, watch, feel, find, etc.）或使役动词（make, have, get, etc.）

● 分词的其他形式

Having cleaned the house, she went on to water the garden.
打扫完房子之后,她又去给花园浇水。

The car *being washed* is not mine.
正在洗的那辆车不是我的。

Having been told what happened, Mary left with sorrow.
被告知所发生的事之后,玛丽伤心地离开了。

Having graduated from college, he went abroad.
从大学毕业后,他出国了。

Having been warned about the pirates, they canceled their trip.
听到有关海盗的警告后,他们取消了行程。

> 表示动作发生在谓语动作之前,用 **having done** 的形式。
> 表示正在发生或与谓语动作同时发生的被动动作,用 **being done** 的形式。

重点及难点 (Key points)

● 现在分词和过去分词的区别

表示动作正在进行 ← 现在分词 → 表示主动

表示动作已经完成 ← 过去分词 → 表示被动

sleeping beauty 睡美人
damaged reputation 受损的名声
The result is really *disappointing*. We all feel *disappointed*.
结果真是令人失望。我们都感到失望。
The man *chosen* to be the astronaut is very handsome.
被选中当宇航员的那个人很英俊。
The man *standing* over there is my cousin.
站在那儿的那个人是我的堂兄。

● 分词的逻辑主语

> 切记：分词的逻辑主语必须与主句主语一致。若不一致时，分词须有自己的主语。

Driving down the road, I saw a kangaroo.
在路上行驶时，我看见了一只袋鼠。
Weather *permitting*, the spaceship will be launched tomorrow evening.
天气允许的话，宇宙飞船将在明晚升空。
Work *done*, he sat down to rest.
活做完了，他坐下来休息。

 应用 (Practice)

I. **Read the following job advertisement. Find all the participles and analyze the roles they play.** (阅读理解下面一则招聘广告，找出所有的分词，并分析其用法。)

    A busy manufacturing company requires an assistant manager for its office administration department. The assistant manager required is to help lead a team of 12 people that deals with the full range of administration tasks, including managing incoming and outgoing correspondence, some personnel duties and ensuring the smooth and efficient operation of the company. Most of the products are exported.

    You will require:
    1. A university degree in business or a related subject.
    2. Five years' experience in a relevant field.
    3. Excellent written and spoken English.
    4. A willingness to work in a high-pressure environment.

II. **Fill in the blanks with the proper forms of the given words.** (用所给词的适当形式填空。)

1. The police started off to search for the (miss) _____ boy.
2. The plan (discuss) _____ now must be kept as a secret.
3. (Not pay) _____ attention, he didn't know what others were talking about.
4. The solider (wound) _____ in the war has become a doctor.
5. Did you notice his hands (shake) _____?
6. When I came back, I found my tape-recorder (steal) _____.
7. (give) _____ more attention, the trees could have grown better.
8. (do) _____ the homework, she went on to listen to the radio.

III. Rewrite the following sentences according to the requirements. (根据要求改写下列句子。)

1. This is the magazine which was sent to me by mail. (改从句为分词结构)
2. The boy who studies very hard is going to Harvard this fall. (改从句为分词结构)
3. There are several points indicated in his speech. (改分词结构为从句)
4. I want to meet the person working on the case. (改分词结构为从句)
5. While he was taking a walk in the street, he saw an accident. (改从句为分词结构)
6. Although she is young, she knows quite a lot. (改从句为分词结构)
7. Compared with the old types, the new machine has a lot of advantages. (改分词结构为从句)
8. When heated, ice will turn into water. (改分词结构为从句)

Unit 15　不定式 (Infinitives)

导入 (Lead-in)

在莎士比亚的这句名言中,斜体部分是一种什么结构？

To be, or *not to be*—that is the question.
生存或毁灭, 这是个必答之问题。

看看下面的句子,想想这种结构可以用在什么地方？有变化形式吗？
To help the poor people of the world is a noble goal.
帮助全世界的穷人是一个崇高的目标。
Kathy wants *to study* with her friends.
凯茜想和她的朋友们一起学习。
I am expecting *to be given* a pay-rise next month.
我期待着下个月提薪。
Wherever she goes, there is a book *to read* in her bag.
无论她去哪儿,包里总有一本要读的书。
To see is *to believe*.
眼见为实。
He asked me *to do* the work with him.
他要我和他一起工作。
Sorry *to have interrupted* you.
对不起,打扰您了。

Unit 15　不定式

讲解 (Explanation)

> "to + 动词原形"这一结构叫动词不定式,是动词的一种非谓语形式,其否定形式为"not to + 动词原形"。在某些情况下 to 可以省略。

● 不定式的功能

To climb Mt. Everest **is** my greatest ambition.
攀登珠穆朗玛峰是我最大的抱负。
To study hard **will increase** your chances of getting a good job.
努力学习会增加你获得好工作的机会。
To sleep **is** the only thing Eli wants after his double shift.
睡觉是艾里下夜班后唯一想做的事。
To restore old cars **is** expensive.
修复旧车很贵。
To stop the car suddenly **can be** dangerous.
突然停车会很危险。

> 不定式结构作主语时,谓语用单数。

（不定式结构作主语时谓语有什么特点？）

The school **promised** *to help* me find an apartment.
学校答应帮我找个公寓。
She **failed** *to explain* the problem clearly.
她没能清楚地解释这个问题。
He **claimed** *to be* an expert.
他声称自己是专家。
We **want** *to visit* all of the historic sites.
我们想去参观所有的古迹。

（什么动词后常接不定式结构作宾语？）

> 接不定式结构作宾语的动词有: want, decide, hope, expect, intend, afford, plan, offer, refuse, promise, etc.

They **invited** us *to have* dinner at their house yesterday.
他们昨天邀请我们去他们家吃晚饭。
You can **ask** him *to wait* for ten minutes.
你可以要求他等十分钟。
I **expect** you *to be* punctual.
我希望你准时。

（什么动词后常接不定式结构作宾语补足语？）

Tell him *not to come* tomorrow.
告诉他明天别来了。

> 接**不定式结构作宾语补足语**的动词主要是表示要求、允许、希望等的动词，如：ask, allow, expect, want, tell, wish, etc.

Her job is *to take* care of the children.
她的工作是照顾孩子。
His dream is *to buy* a luxurious car.
他的梦想是买一辆豪华汽车。
What Tom wants now is *to find* a good job.
汤姆现在想要的是找个好工作。
To work is *to earn* a living.
工作是谋生的手段。

> 观察这些句子的主语有什么特点。

> **不定式作表语**时，主语一般是 job, plan, purpose, duty, aim, dream, wish, hobby 等名词，或 what 引导的主语从句，或不定式。

The language *to suit* the occasion is the best.
适合场合的语言是最好的。
The first attempt *to build* the Panama Canal ended in failure.
修建巴拿马运河的第一次尝试以失败结束。
He is looking for a room *to live* in.
他在寻找住的地方。
There is nothing *to worry* about.
没什么可担心的。
The best way *to improve* your English is to practice a lot.
提高英语最好的办法是多练。

> 注意这些句子中不定式的位置。

> **不定式作定语**放在所修饰的名词之后。

To win, you need the highest number of points.
要想获胜，你需要有最高的得分。
I nodded *to show* respect.
我点头以示尊敬。
To get there on time, you need to leave now.
要想按时到的话，你现在就需要出发了。
It's good *to see* you.
很高兴见到你。

> 在句中不定式分别作的是什么状语？

130

They were happy *to hear* the news.
听到这个消息他们很高兴。
I'm too tired to *continue*.
我太累了，无法继续下去。
He hurried to the station only *to find* the train had left.
他匆匆忙忙赶到车站，却发现火车已经离开了。

> **不定式作状语**，可表示目的、原因和结果。

☞ 思考：句子成分中只有一种成分不能由不定式来担任，是什么成分？

● 不定式的其他形式

The woman seemed *to have been crying*.
这个妇女好像一直在哭。
He pretended *to have been painting* all day.
他假装整天都在画画。
I'd really like *to be swimming* in a nice cool pool right now.
我现在特别想在一个凉爽的游泳池里游泳。
I happened *to be waiting* for the bus when the accident happened.
事故发生时，我刚好在等公共汽车。
He pretended *to have seen* the film.
他假装看过这部电影。
The building was said *to have been* completely *destroyed*.
据说那幢大楼被完全毁掉了。
Everyone wants *to be rewarded* for his efforts.
每个人都想付出的努力能带来回报。

	主动	被动	用法
一般式	to do	to be done	不定式表示的动作发生在谓语动作之后，或同时发生。
进行式	to be doing		不定式表示的动作与谓语动作同时发生。
完成式	to have done	to have been done	不定式表示的动作发生在谓语动作之前。
完成进行式	to have been doing		不定式表示的动作发生在谓语动作之前，并持续到谓语动作发生。

(do 表示动词原形，doing 表示动词现在分词，done 表示动词过去分词)

重点及难点 (Key points)

● 不定式与形式主语和形式宾语 - it

> 不定式结构作主语或宾语时，如果太长，则用 it 来作形式主语或形式宾语，而把不定式放到句子后面。

It is very difficult *to remember* so many words in a short time.
在短时间内记这么多单词很难。

It is a good idea *to save* money for a rainy day.
存些钱以备不时之需是个好主意。

It is foolish *to waste* time in class.
在课上浪费时间很愚蠢。

It takes half an hour *to get* there by bike.
骑车去那儿要花半个小时。

I found **it** impossible *to accept* the view.
我发现不可能接受这个观点。

Do you think **it** necessary **for** a student *to learn* a foreign language?
你认为学生学一门外语是必要的吗？

It is probably a good idea **for** parents *to allow* teenagers to study in groups.
父母允许十多岁的孩子在一起学习或许是个好主意。

> 当不定式的逻辑主语与句子主语不一致时，不定式的逻辑主语可由 for 引出。

● 不定式省略 to

> 不定式作宾语补足语时，若谓语动词是感官动词 (see, watch, hear, feel, notice, etc.) 或使役动词 (make, let, have)，则不定式省略 to。

Of course we want to **see** him *succeed*.
我们当然想看到他成功了。

I'll **have** him *repair* the car.
我会让他把车修好的。

The music always **makes** me *feel* happy.
这个音乐总是让我感到开心。

Nobody **noticed** him *enter* the room.
没有人注意到他进入房间。

> **注意：**若这些感官动词和使役动词用于被动语态时，其后的不定式要补上在主动语态中省略的 to。

The man **was seen** *to enter* the hotel.
有人看见那个人进了这家饭店。
I **was made** *to love* her.
我生来就是为了爱她。

● 特殊疑问代词或副词 + 不定式

> 不定式前加特殊疑问代词或副词，在句中作主语、宾语或表语。why 后面的不定式不带 to。

I really don't know *what to say*.
我真不知道该说什么。
Where to go is yet to be decided.
去哪儿还没有决定下来。
What they want to know is *how to solve* the problem.
他们想知道的是如何解决这个问题。
I couldn't decide *which one to choose*.
我决定不了选哪一个。

● 介词 but, except, besides + 不定式

> 两种情况：如果这些介词前有 do，则其后的不定式不带 to；如果这些介词前没有 do，则其后的不定式要带 to。

I couldn't **do** anything but *sit* there.
我什么都不能做，只有坐在那儿。
He had no choice but *to quit* his job.
除了辞职，他没有其他选择。

 应用 (Practice)

I. Read the following quotations. Point out the infinitives.（阅读下列名人名言，指出不定式。）

   "It is better to keep your mouth closed and let people think you are a fool than to open it and remove all doubt." (Mark Twain)

"Half our life is spent trying to find something to do with the time we have rushed through life trying to save." (Will Rogers)

"A celebrity is a person who works hard all his life to become well known, then wears dark glasses to avoid being recognized." (Fred Allen)

"To educate a man in mind and not in morals is to educate a menace to society." (President Theodore Roosevelt)

"It's not that I'm afraid to die, I just don't want to be there when it happens." (Woody Allen)

"It's always easier to learn something than to use what you've learned." (Chaim Potok, *The Promise*)

"I intend to live forever. So far, so good." (Steven Wright)

"I didn't mean to be a role model. I just speak my truth. I guess speaking from your heart really creates a huge impact, and if I can encourage people to do that, then I would love to be a role model. If I could encourage people to use their voices loudly, then that's my reward." (Margaret Cho)

II. **Choose from the four choices the most appropriate one to complete the sentences.** (从四个选项中选择最合适的完成句子。)

1. After twelve years abroad, William came back only _____ his hometown severely damaged in an earthquake.
   A. to find   B. finding
   C. to have found   D. to be finding

2. I am sorry _____ you so much trouble.
   A. to have given   B. to have been given
   C. to be given   D. to giving

3. They seemed _____ before I came.
   A. to leave   B. to have left
   C. to have been leaving   D. to have been left

4. It is important _____ you to get there in time.
   A. that   B. for
   C. of   D. whether

5. Do you consider _____ necessary to tell him?
   A. it   B. it would be
   C. it to be   D. it as being

6. It was so noisy outside that the speaker could hardly _____.
   A. make himself hear   B. make the audience hearing him
   C. make the audience hear him   D. make the audience heard

7. Because air pollution has been greatly reduced, this city is still _____.
   A. a good place to live   B. a good place for living in
   C. a good place to be lived in   D. a good place to live in

8. Do you know _____ a cake?
   A. to making   B. how to make
   C. making   D. about making
9. The students expected there _____ more time to enjoy themselves.
   A. is   B. being
   C. have been   D. to be
10. I didn't know _____ him or not.
    A. whether to visit   B. if to visit
    C. to visit   D. that if I should visit
11. She is going to town _____.
    A. to repair her radio   B. to have repaired her radio
    C. to have her radio repaired   D. for repairing her radio
12. Scientists think that laser _____ one of the most useful tools in use today.
    A. be   B. to be
    C. being   D. is
13. This organization is reported _____ twenty years ago.
    A. be set up   B. being set up
    C. to have been set up   D. to be set up
14. It is better to die on one's feet than _____.
    A. live on one's knees   B. living one's knees
    C. on one's knees   D. to live on one's knees
15. The building is said _____ in a fire three years ago.
    A. to damage   B. to be damaged
    C. to have been damaged   D. to being damaged

III. **Rewrite the following sentences, using infinitives instead of clauses.（改写下列句子，把从句改为不定式结构。）**
   1. There are still a lot of problems that we need to solve.
   2. They signed an agreement that they should increase cooperation between their companies.
   3. I'm sorry that I should tell you the bad news.
   4. She was pleased when she found her son doing so well at school.
   5. I'm worrying about what I should say.
   6. When we will meet them has not been decided.
   7. We don't know where we should go.
   8. They are so tired that they can't continue.
   9. I expect that you come here on time.
   10. They insisted that they should be rewarded for their efforts.

Unit 16 动名词 (Gerunds)

 导入 (Lead-in)

斜体部分的词就是动名词。它让你想起了什么词？

"*Feeling* gratitude and not *expressing* it is like *wrapping* a present and not *giving* it."
(William A. Ward)

再看看其他的例句：
Swimming is fun.
游泳很有意思。
Tom enjoys *swimming* a lot.
汤姆很喜欢游泳。
He gives *swimming* all his time and energy.
他把所有的时间和精力都放在游泳上。
He is devoted to *swimming*.
他全心致力于游泳。

☞ 思考：动名词跟动词和名词有关系吗？动名词跟现在分词有什么异同？

 讲解 (Explanation)

动名词兼有动词的含义和名词的功能，其形式与现在分词一样，即"动词＋ing"，否定形式是 not＋动词＋ing。

☞ 思考：有名词功能的动名词在句中能作什么成分呢？

动名词的功能

Playing football takes up too much of his time.
踢足球占了他太多的时间。

Smoking costs a lot of money.
抽烟要花很多钱。

It's no use **arguing** with him.
跟他争辩没用。

Walking is a good form of exercise.
走路是一种很好的锻炼形式。

> 动名词结构可在句中作主语。

He denied **stealing** anything.
他否认偷了东西。

I can't understand **neglecting** children like that.
对孩子那样毫不经心，我不能理解。

Would you mind **waiting** a little longer?
你介意再等一会儿吗？

We are looking forward to **seeing** you.
我们盼望着见到你。

He has been dreaming of **traveling** around the world.
他一直梦想着环游世界。

> 动名词结构可在句中作宾语，既可作动词宾语，也可作介词宾语。

That is ballet **dancing**.
这就是芭蕾舞。

His first job was **washing** dishes in a restaurant.
他的第一份工作是在餐馆洗盘子。

The only thing she likes to do is **reading** novels.
她唯一爱做的事是看小说。

The best thing for your health is **not smoking**.
对你健康最好的事是不吸烟。

> 动名词结构可在句中作表语。

> 提示：动名词与现在分词虽同形，但作用不一样。动名词在句子中起名词作用，而现在分词在句子中的作用与形容词和副词相当。

动名词的其他形式

Being involved in the scandal made the small town become famous overnight.
陷入丑闻使这个小镇一夜成名。

He tried to escape **being punished.**
他设法逃避惩罚。

He was afraid of **being left** at home alone.
他害怕一个人留在家里。

Having been to South Korea helped her learn the language.
去过韩国有助于她学习韩语。

I appreciate **having been given** the opportunity to study abroad two years ago.
我很感激两年前给我出国学习的机会。

	主动	被动	用法
一般式	doing	being done	动名词所表示的动作与谓语动作同时发生，也可在谓语动作之前或之后发生，有时可能没有明确的先后关系。
完成式	having done	having been done	动名词所表示的动作先于谓语动作发生。

(do 表示动词原形，doing 表示动名词，done 表示动词过去分词)

重点及难点 (Key points)

动名词与不定式

动名词和不定式在句中都能作主语、表语和宾语。问题是什么时候该用动名词，什么时候该用不定式。

> 作主语或表语时，**动名词**表示的是经常性的、一般的动作，而**不定式**表示的是可能的、潜在的、将发生的动作。

Learning is important.
学习很重要。

To get there by bike will take us half an hour.
骑自行车去那儿要花我们半个小时。

Unit 16　动名词

Reading helps you learn English.
阅读有助于学习英语。
To study in Harvard University is his dream.
上哈佛大学是他的梦想。
The most important thing is **learning**.
最重要的事是学习。
His dream is **to study** in Harvard University.
他的梦想是上哈佛大学。

> 作动词宾语时，有三种情况：1. 约定俗成，有些动词后只能跟动名词，有些动词后只能跟不定式；2. 有些动词后既能跟动名词，又能跟不定式，但意思差别很大；3. 有些动词后既能跟动名词，又能跟不定式，而且意思差别不大。

情况 1：

常见的只接动名词的动词：admit, avoid, appreciate, can't help, consider, delay, enjoy, finish, keep, imagine, mind, miss, postpone, practice, recommend, resist, risk, suggest, etc.

常见的只接不定式的动词：agree, appear, arrange, decide, demand, deserve, fail, hesitate, hope, intend, manage, offer, plan, refuse, seem, tend, vow, wait, want, wish, etc.

He admitted **cheating** on the test.
他承认考试作弊。
I can't help **thinking** about it.
我忍不住老想这件事。
Jim recommended **taking** the ship.
吉姆建议坐船。
David agreed **to help** us.
戴维同意帮我们。
The customer demanded **to speak** to the manager.
顾客要求见经理。
We failed to persuade him **to work** with us.
我们没能说服他和我们一起工作。

情况 2：

既能接动名词，又能接不定式的动词	后接动名词 doing	后接不定式 to do
forget	忘记做过某事（事已做）	忘记去做某事（事没做）
stop	停止做这事	停下来去做（另一件事）
remember	记得做过某事（事已做）	记住要去做某事（未做）
regret	后悔、遗憾做过某事（事已做）	对要做的事遗憾（未做）
try	尝试、试着做某事	企图、努力做某事
mean	意味着做某事	打算、有意要做某事

I forgot **reading** the book when I was a kid.
我忘了小时候看过这本书。

I forgot **to call** you this morning.
我今天上午忘了给你打电话了。

He stopped **talking**.
他停止了说话。

He stopped **to talk** with me.
他停下来，跟我说话。

I remember **sending** you an email yesterday.
我记得昨天给你发了一封电子邮件。

I'll remember **to send** you an email.
我会记着给你发电子邮件的。

I regretted **being** late to the interview.
我后悔面试时去晚了。

We regret **to tell** you that the meeting was canceled.
我们遗憾地告诉你，会议取消了。

I didn't mean **to hurt** your feeling.
我没想伤害你的感情。

Does retirement mean **doing** nothing?
退休意味着什么都不做吗?

情况 3：

> 动词如 like, hate, prefer, love 等既可以接动名词作宾语，又可以接不定式作宾语，且意思差别不大，动名词表示的是经常性的、一般的动作，而不定式表示的是可能的、潜在的、将发生的动作。

Cathy likes **reading**.
凯茜喜欢阅读。

Cathy likes **to read** some magazines.
凯茜想看些杂志。
Ben prefers **having** dinner at home.
本喜欢在家吃晚饭。
Ben prefers **to have** dinner at home.
本想在家吃晚饭。

● 动名词的逻辑主语

> 动名词的逻辑主语可用形容词性物主代词(my, his, her, our, their, its)，或名词所有格来表示。

The rain prevented **his** *coming*.
下雨使他不能来。
Excuse **my** *opening* your letter by mistake.
原谅我不慎把你的信拆开。
My mother's *cooking* is famous in my hometown.
我妈妈的厨艺在我家乡很有名。
Jake's *driving* scares me.
杰克开车让我害怕。

应用 (Practice)

I. Read the following paragraphs. Point out the gerunds. (阅读下面的段落，指出动名词。)

　　Some foreign business people have spent decades working with Chinese companies. But others are newcomers. To many Westerners, China is the ultimate in exotic locations. So the chances are that your Western business contact will have a lot more on the agenda for his visit to China than looking around factories and discussing products.

　　You can probably build an excellent relationship by understanding that these people are very keen on seeing something of "the real China". You can find out what they are interested in by the simple method of asking them. Some of them may enjoy half an hour chatting with the elderly. Even a simple walk around the streets can be much valued.

II. Fill in the blanks with the proper forms of the words given. (用所给词的适当形式填空。)

1. Yesterday my mother meant _____ (make) pizza, but I didn't have time.
2. My friend postponed _____ (go) abroad.

3. Do you always have breakfast before _____ (go) to school?
4. Do you object to _____ (work) overtime.
5. Mark is considering _____ (buy) a new house.
6. She quit _____ (complain) about _____ (be) unemployed and decided _____ (create) her own job.
7. On the way home from work, he stopped _____ (buy) some groceries.
8. She dreamed of _____ (accept) to the famous university.
9. The problem is far from _____ (solve).
10. I avoid _____ (use) my cell phone when other people are in the room.

III. **Combine the two sentences by changing the first one into a gerund or gerund phrase.** (把前一个句子变成动名词或动名词结构，把两句合为一句。)

例：He plays football. It takes up too much of his time.
→ Playing football takes up too much of his time.

1. They may lose the match. They are afraid of it.
2. She works the night shift. She doesn't mind it.
3. You have to take the examination. It is the only way to get into the school.
4. People brush teeth twice a day. This is what all dentists recommend.
5. We will go out at the weekend. We are looking forward to it.
6. We learnt foreign culture. This helped us to communicate with foreigners.
7. He collects stamps. His hobby is that.
8. I have the opportunity to take part in the project. I really appreciate it.
9. They have to participate in six months of field studies. The course requires that.

分词、不定式和动名词

I. In this section, there are 10 incomplete sentences. You are required to complete each one by deciding on the most appropriate word or words from the 4 choices marked A, B, C and D.

1. The May Day Holiday _____ over, we must now get down to work.
   A. be   B. being   C. to have been   D. to be
2. _____ to find the proper job, he decided to give up job-hunting in this city.
   A. Failed   B. Being failed   C. To fail   D. Having failed
3. The proposal _____, we'll have to make another decision about when to start the project.
   A. accepted   B. accepting   C. to accept   D. be accepted
4. The policeman kept his eyes _____ on the screen of the computer to identify the criminal's footprints.
   A. fixed   B. fixing   C. being fixed   D. to fix
5. _____ that Bob had got promoted, his friends came to congratulate him.
   A. Heard   B. Having heard   C. Hear   D. To hear
6. The professor, _____ as a splendid speaker, was warmly received by the students.
   A. known   B. to be known   C. knowing   D. having known
7. _____ tired of Tom's all-talk-no-action attitude, Julia decided to do the job all by herself.
   A. To get   B. To have got   C. Getting   D. Have got
8. After _____ for the job, you will be required to take a language test.
   A. being interviewed   B. being interviewing   C. interviewing   D. having interviewed
9. The City of London, _____ repeatedly in 1940 and 1941, lost many of its famous churches.
   A. bombed   B. to bomb   C. bombing   D. having bombed
10. _____ traveling expenses rising a lot, Mrs. White had to change all her plans for the tour.
    A. Since   B. As for   C. By   D. With
11. _____ how to deal with the trouble of the computer, Martin had to ask his brother for help.
    A. Not know   B. Not known   C. Not to know   D. Not knowing
12. It's said that the agreement _____ between the two companies last month will become effective from May 1st.
    A. to sign   B. signed   C. to be signed   D. signing
13. I stayed up all night _____ to find a new solution to the problem.
    A. trying   B. have tried   C. try   D. tried

14. _____ with the developed countries, some African countries are left far behind in terms of people's living standard.
    A. Compare   B. To compare   C. Compared   D. Comparing
15. _____, we went swimming in the river.
    A. The day being very hot   B. It was a very hot day
    C. The day was very hot   D. Being a very hot day
16. I have found some articles _____ the harmful effects of drinking.
    A. being concerned   B. concerned
    C. to concern   D. concerning
17. At the international conference, the famous scientist gave an excellent report _____ on his recent experiment.
    A. basing   B. based   C. to be based   D. to base
18. I'm still unable to make myself _____ in the discussion, which worries me a lot.
    A. to be understood   B. understanding   C. understood   D. understand
19. Thousands of products _____ from crude oil are now in daily use.
    A. to make   B. be made   C. making   D. made
20. Are you going to fix the car yourself, or are you going to have it _____?
    A. fixing   B. to fix   C. fix   D. fixed
21. If _____ in the fridge, the fruit can remain fresh for more than a week.
    A. keeping   B. be kept   C. kept   D.
22. _____, he can quickly find out what's wrong with the medicine.
    A. Having been well trained   B. Having well trained
    C. To be well trained   D. To have been well trained
23. While _____ in London, the young engineer picked up some English.
    A. staying   B. stay   C. stayed   D. to stay
24. _____ Annie's glass, I apologized to her.
    A. To break   B. Breaking   C. Having broken   D. Break
25. She didn't know _____ to express her ideas clearly when she was invited to speak at a meeting.
    A. where   B. why   C. what   D. how
26. I felt so embarrassed that I couldn't do anything but _____ there when I first met my personal boss.
    A. to sit   B. sitting   C. sat   D. sit
27. Jane always enjoys _____ to popular music at home on Friday evenings.
    A. listening   B. being listening C. to be listening D. to listen
28. There are so many dresses there that I really don't know _____ to choose.
    A. whether   B. when   C. which   D. why
29. Because of the reduction of air pollution, this city now is a good place _____.
    A. where to live   B. which to live   C. to live   D. to be lived

30. He was very sorry _____ her at the airport.
    A. not to meet   B. to not meet   C. to have not met   D. not to have met
31. She gave up her job as a nurse because she found the children too difficult _____.
    A. look after   B. to look after   C. looking after   D. be looked after
32. More and more trucks are seen _____ between these two towns these days.
    A. run   B. to run   C. be running   D. being run
33. The father was delighted to hear the child _____ that.
    A. to say   B. to have said   C. say   D. said
34. _____ is quite difficult for Mary to pass the interview.
    A. What   B. This   C. That   D. It
35. You'd better _____ the whole article at once.
    A. copy   B. copying   C. to copy   D copied
36. It cost her a lot of money, but she doesn't regret _____ a year traveling around the world.
    A. to have spent   B. to spend   C. spent   D. spending
37. He doesn't feel like _____ a picnic in the park this weekend, and he suggested watching the football match instead.
    A. have   B. to have   C. having   D. had

II. **There are 10 incomplete statements here. You should fill in each blank with the proper form of the word given in the brackets.**

1. Most of the people (invite) _____ to the dinner party yesterday were my friends.
2. Last night we all went to the cinema, because the film was very (excite) _____.
3. We were shocked to find that the man (come) _____ towards us was carrying a gun.
4. (impress) _____ by the young man's good qualifications, they offered him a job in their firm.
5. We regret to inform you that we no longer manufacture the product you ar (interest) _____ in.
6. The tall building (complete) _____ last month is our new classroom building.
7. The children (play) _____ the violin over there will go on the stage next week.
8. (watch) _____ by a crowd of people, Charles felt embarrassed and couldn't say a word.
9. (Take) _____ the financial difficulties into consideration, we'd better put off the plan until next year.
10. When (ask) _____ why he came to the exhibition, he said that he had been interested in oiling painting for years.
11. If all the people agree on the (suggest) _____ plan, we shall hold the sports meet at the end of this month.
12. (Give) _____ more instructions, the students would have done the exercises much better.
13. In the middle of the room there was a Christmas tree (decorate) _____ with colored lights and glass balls.

14. (Judge) _____ from last year's experience, the coach knows he should not expect too much of his team.
15. When he was in hospital, the nurse had his temperature (take) _____ every four hours.
16. His book was much better than those (write) _____ so far on this subject.
17. Give the application to the man (sit) _____ at the desk, please.
18. While (cross) _____ the street, I saw someone waving to me.
19. I noticed that there was a man (draw) _____ pictures on the ground.
20. There was a stranger (stand) _____ at the door.
21. The chairman should raise his voice in order to make himself (hear) _____.
22. I saw the man (knock) _____ down by a car in the street.
23. If you intend (visit) _____ the National garden, please contact me soon.
24. The manager promised (get) _____ me a position in his company.
25. They stopped (search) _____ for the missing plane as the weather was very rough.
26. My secretary asked me if I had anything else for her (type) _____ before she left.
27. We formally invited the General Manager of the panda Group (attend) _____ our opening ceremony.
28. The nurse told the visitors (not speak) _____ so loudly as to disturb the patients.
29. When she was very young, my sister already knew where (put) _____ her toys and dolls.
30. The global average air temperature is believed (rise) _____ in the near future.
31. I prefer (live) _____ in the country rather than in a city.
32. Mark was a little upset, for the manager didn't allow him (take) _____ his holiday the following week.
33. No student is supposed (spend) _____ so much money in school in a week.
34. It is never too late for anyone (learn) _____.
35. When I called her on the phone, she pretended (not know) _____ me.
36. I asked him not (say) _____ anything about our contract until the end of the month.
37. We all felt excited when China succeeded in (launch) _____ its first manned spaceship.
38. For those foreign students who are interested in (learn) _____ Chinese, the university offers a Chinese training program every summer.
39. A guest in this hotel accused one of the hotel staff of (steal) _____ his money.
40. There's no use (bargain) _____ any more. It's fixed price.
41. In some parts of this city, missing a bus means (wait) _____ for another hour.
42. We appreciate (work) _____ with him, because he has a good sense of humor.
43. He has to check the (spell) _____ of a difficult word before he uses it.
44. The teacher didn't mind (help) _____ the students in her spare time.
45. Some American businessmen in China are spending a lot of time in (learn) _____ Chinese.
46. Please remember (lock) _____ the door when you leave.
47. When Jenny came to Britain, she had to get used to (drive) _____ on the left.

48. Did you have difficulties (get) _____ a visa to Britain?
49. I don't mind (have) _____ a dog in the house so long as it's clean and it doesn't smell.
50. Hearing the bell ring, the students stopped (joke) _____ with each other.
51. The girls happily look forward to (see) _____ the movie star at the party.
52. The children from the U.S. got used to (eat) _____ Chinese food quite soon.

Unit 17　冠词 (Articles)

 导入 (Lead-in)

这三句话的含义相同吗？
如相同为什么他们使用
不同的限定词？

马是一种有用的动物。
A horse is an useful animal.
The horse is an useful animal.
Horses are useful animals.

看看下面的句子,想想斜体部分的词在句子中起什么作用,有什么不同。
The doctor told him to take *the* medicine three times *a* day.
医生叫他每天吃三次药。
Take *the* letters to *the* post office.
把信拿到邮局。
The simplest kind of advertising is *the* classified ads.
最简单的广告是分类广告。

 讲解 (Explanation)

冠词是放在名词前,用来说明名词的词。英语的冠词有两种:不定冠词(indefinite article)和定冠词(definite article)。

a 和 an 有什么区别

● 不定冠词的用法

不定冠词表示泛指: a 和 an
a 与 an 的用法

148

Unit 17　冠词

表示任何事物的种类，以区别其他的种类。	She is **a** language teacher. 她是个语言教师。
表示数量"一"，但数量概念比 one 弱	Some people think of a family as **a** mother, **a** father, and their children. 有的人把家庭理解为一位母亲，一位父亲及其子女。
表示一类人或物，此用法和定冠词 the 相同	A compass is **an** instrument for showing direction. 指南针是一种指示方向的仪器。
表示"某个"、"任何一个"	**A** library could hardly be used if the books were kept in random order. 任何一家图书馆，如果它的藏书没有固定的规律就很难得到利用。

> a 用在辅音音素前，an 用在元音音素前，如 a car, a college student, a university, an apple, an effective way.

☞ 思考：有些抽象名词或物质名词为什么也会和 a/an 连用呢？

● **定冠词 the 的用法**

表示上文提到的人或事物	There is a girl and an old man standing at the bus stop. I think **the** man must be the girl's father. 有一个女孩和一位老人站在汽车站。我想那老人一定是女孩的父亲。
用于带有限定性修饰语的名词之前	This is **the** house where my father once lived. 这是我父亲曾经住过的那间房子。 **The** train to Beijing is on platform 4. 开往北京的火车停靠 4 站台。
用于天体、方位、左右、世上独有的事物之前	**The** moon is about 239,000 miles away from **the** earth. 月球离地球约有 239,000 英里。 **The** sun rises in the east. 太阳在东方升起。
在形容词最高级、序数词前面	This is **the** most moving story I have ever heard. 这是我听过的最感人的故事。 **The** second tax is for the state government. 第二种税收是州政府征收的。
在某些河流、海洋、山脉、群岛、海峡、海湾等专有名词前	**the** Yangtze 长江 **the** Red Sea 红海 **the** Atlantic Ocean 大西洋
某些由普通名词和其他词构成的专有名词前	**the** People's Republic of China 中华人民共和国 **the** United Nations 联合国 **the** Great Hall of the People 人民大会堂
某些形容词前，表示一类人	**the** poor 穷人 **the** rich 富人 **the** sick 病人
在某些习惯用语的名词前	in **the** morning 在上午 by **the** way 顺便说 on **the** whole 总的来说

● 零冠词

人名、地名等专有名词前不加冠词	George Washington 乔治华盛顿 India 印度 Hong Kong 香港
三餐与球类名词前	after breakfast play basketball
泛指的不可数名词前和表示一般概念的复数名词前	Social scientists study families. 社会科学研究家庭。 Diamond are made from carbon 金刚石是由碳元素构成的。

> 有没有不加冠词的情况呢？

☞ 思考：表示称呼、官衔、职位的名词前是否使用冠词，使用什么样的冠词？

重点及难点 (Key points)

- 有些抽象名词和物质名词也和 a/an 连用，表示一次、一种、一场等。
  It's **a** pleasure to talk with you. 和你谈话很高兴。
  Longjing is **a** famous Chinese tea. 龙井是一种著名的中国茶。

- 在表示身体部位的名词前使用 the。
  She caught me by **the** arm. 她抓住了我的手臂。
  He hit me in **the** face. 他打了我的脸。

- 表示称呼、官衔、职位的名词前不加冠词。
  She is Chairman of the meeting. 她是会议的主席。
  In 1860, Abraham Lincoln was elected President of the US. 1860 年，林肯被选为美国总统。

应用 (Practice)

Choose the correct answer（选择合适的答案）

1. John likes playing _____.
   A. basketball   B. the basketball   C. a basketball   D. basketballs

2. _____ is very important in daily life.
   A. Honesty   B. The honesty   C. An honesty   D. Honest

3. Connie: "What musical instrument do you play?"
   A. Piano　　　B. A piano　　　C. Pianos　　　D. The piano
4. A young man cannot have _____.
   A. experience of world　　　B. experience of the world
   C. the experience of world　　　D. the experience of the world
5. Wooden houses _____ easily.
   A. catch a fire　　B. catch fire　　C. catch the fire　　D. catch fires
6. _____ Mr. Black came to visit you a moment ago. He was in _____ hurry.
   A. /— the　　B. /— a　　C. The — a　　D. A — the
7. People are now realizing the importance of treating _____ kindly.
   A. old　　B. the old　　C. elderly　　D. the elder
8. If you want to lose _____ weight, you'd better be on _____ diet and do exercises regularly.
   A. the — /　　B. / — the　　C. / — /　　D. the — the
9. Every Sunday, my mother asks me to go to _____ church.
   A. /　　B. the　　C. a　　D. an
10. Applicants must have _____ good knowledge of _____ maths.
    A. / — a　　B. a — the　　C. a — /　　D. / — /
11. _____ usually go to church every Sunday.
    A. The Brown　　B. A Brown　　C. Browns　　D. The Browns
12. The train is running fifty miles _____.
    A. an hour　　B. one hour　　C. the hour　　D. a hour
13. A new teacher was sent to the village in place of _____ one who had retired.
    A. a　　B. the　　C. an　　D. its
14. I like drinking _____ tea and Longjing is _____ wonderful tea.
    A. the, a　　B. /, a　　C. /, /　　D. a, a
15. Lesson 4 is _____ most difficult lesson, but it isn't _____ most difficult lesson in Book Ⅱ.
    A. the, the　　B. a, a　　C. the, a　　D. a, the
16. In China, _____ bicycle is _____ popular means of transportation.
    A. the, a　　B. a, /　　C. the, the　　D. a, the
17. I played _____ tennis with Mary yesterday evening. It was really _____ enjoyable game. We stopped playing only after _____ sun had set.
    A. a, a, /　　B. the, an, the　　C. the, /, the　　D. /, an, the
18. _____ Europe and _____ America are separated by _____ Atlantic Ocean.
    A. /, /, the　　B. the, the, the　　C. /, /, /　　D. the, the, /
19. He was elected _____ Chairman of the meeting.
    A. the　　B. a　　C. as　　D. /
20. Pay special attention to the idioms of _____ English language.
    A. the　　B. a　　C. as　　D. /

Unit 18　介词 (Prepositions)

导入 (Lead-in)

下列的斜体部分词的含义都有什么不同？

The ship sailed
- *on* the sea.
- *out of* the harbor.
- *into* the harbor.
- *under* the bridge.
- *across* the Atlantic.
- *down* the river.
- *up* the river.
- *against* the wind.
- *for* Shanghai.
- *to* New York.

看看下面的句子，想想斜体部分的词在句子中起什么作用。

The skyscraper *in the distance* is a five-star hotel.
远处的摩天大楼是五星级酒店。

The decision is *of great importance* to me.
这个决定对我很重要。

She left *on or about* the eighth of May.
她五月八号离开。

He is 200 dollars *in the red* this month.
他这个月亏损了 200 美元。

My house stands *against* the church.
我的房子正对着教堂。

☞ 思考：介词能否单独作句子成分呢？

 讲解 (Explanation)

> 介词不单独做句子成分，后面跟名词、代词、数词、副词、短语、从句等作它的宾语，构成介词短语。

☞ 思考：介词在句中都作什么样的句子成分？

● **介词短语的功能**

Everybody understood **except** me.
除我之外，大家都理解了。
She seated the baby **on** her knees.
她让宝宝坐在她的双腿上。

> 介词短语可作状语，通常位于句首或句尾，表时间、地点、原因、结果、方式、比较等。

They have rented a flat **of** three rooms.
他们租了一套三居室的公寓。
The lady **in** red is my sister-in-law.
穿红衣服的那位女士是我的嫂子。

> 介词短语可作定语，通常在所修饰的名词后面，作后置定语。

Sally is **in** the language lab with Tom.
萨利和汤姆在语音室。
What he said is **of** great help to learners of English.
他刚才的话对英语学习者很有帮助。

> 介词短语可作表语。

What makes you **in** such a hurry?
什么事使你这样匆忙？
The duty of the police is to keep the country **in** order.
警察的职责是维持国家秩序。

> 介词短语可作宾语补足语。

153

● 介词短语的构成

> 观察这些介词短语，想想介词后面接的是什么词。

along the road 沿着这条路
as an engineer 作为一名工程师
before lunch 午饭前
in front of the house 在房屋前
according to the passage 根据这篇短文
due to the failure 由于故障

> 介词 + 名词

beside us 在我们旁边
for them 为了他们
except him 除他之外
instead of her 代替她
on behalf of us all 代表我们全体

> 介词 + 代词

on 21st, May 在 5 月 21 日
at six 6 点钟
plus 16 加 16
from 10 to 20 从 10 到 20

> 介词 + 数词

without paying any taxes 没有交税
upon hearing the news 一听消息
instead of staying at home 不呆在家里

> 介词 + 动名词

about how he worked at the company 关于他在该公司的工作情况
from what he said 从他所说的情况
on how to improve the efficiency 关于如何提高效率

> 介词 + 疑问代词引导的从句 / 疑问代词 + 不定式短语

重点及难点 (Key points)

● 介词辨析

> **in, at 表示地点的区别**：at 表示某个"点"，in 强调某个"范围"以内。此外，at 用于表示在某一单位、机关，较抽象；in 则较具体，往往与建筑物有一定的关系。

He works **at** the post office.
她在邮局上班。
We were sheltering from the rain **in** the post office.
我们在邮局里避雨。
He is studying **at** Peking University.
他在北京大学读书。
The old professor lives **in** Peking University.
这位老教授住在北京大学里。

> **on, over, above 表示地点的区别**：on 表示一物放在令一物上面，两者紧贴在一起；over 表示一种垂直悬空的上下关系，即"在……—上方"；above 表示一般的"高于……"，"在……之上"。

The book is **on** the table.
书在桌子上。
Is there any bridge **over** the river?
河上有桥吗？
There was an electric clock **above** his bed.
他床头曾经有只电子钟。

> **under，below 的区别**：under 和 below 分别是 over 和 above 的反义词，因此 under 表示垂直的上下关系，即"在……下方"，below 表示"低于……"，"在……之下"。

They were seen **under** the tree.
有人看到他们在树下。
Shall I write my name **on**, **above** or **below** the line.
我该把名字写在线上，还是线的上下方？

> **after, behind 的区别**：after 多用于表时间先后，behind 多表位置或方向的前后。强调先后顺序时，两者意义接近。

She stood **behind** a tree.
他站在一棵树后。
We shall leave **after** breakfast.
我们早饭后动身。
Shut the door **after/ behind** you.
进来后关上门。

> **across, through, over, past 的区别**：across 着重于"从一头或一边到令一头或令一边"；through 强调"穿越"；over 表示"上方越过"；past 表示从"面前经过"。

She went **across** the street to make some purchases.
她穿过街道去购物。
The sunlight was coming in **through** the window.
阳光透过窗户照进来了。
He failed to go **over** the mountain; he had to go around it.
他没能翻过这座山，不得不绕过去。
Someone has just gone **past** the window.
刚有人从窗前走过。

> **in, after 表示时间的区别**：in 表示从现在时间角度所指的"将来"，后接表示一段时间的词；after 表示从过去时间角度所指的"之后"，后接表示某一时刻或某种活动的词。

Dick is leaving for Huston **in** two days.
迪克将于两天后前往休斯敦。
We had to take a taxi home **after** the party.
派对结束后我们只好打的回家。
Citizens were not allowed to go out shortly **after** seven in the evening.
晚上一过七点，市民们就不准外出。

> **at, in, on 表示时间的区别**：at 表示确切的时间，in 表示一天中的某段时间，on 表示某一天或星期几。但是，如果说某日的早、中、晚时需用 on 代替 in。

I have to get up **at** five tomorrow.
明天我必须五点起床。

156

I'll meet you in the coffee bar **at** eight.
八点整我们在咖啡馆里见。
I study **in** the evening.
我晚上学习。
See you **on** Sunday morning.
星期日上午见。
I saw her off at the airport **on** a cold winter evening.
在一个寒冷冬天的晚上,我去机场送他。
Usually I'm free **on** Sundays.
通常我星期天有空。
We're giving her a dinner party **on** her birthday.
我们准备为她举行一个生日派对。

 应用 (Practice)

I. **Fill in each of the blanks in the following sentences with an appropriate preposition.**

1. A modern woman usually does two jobs instead _____ one.
2. We must remember that it is the intelligent application of technology that will lead us _____ success.
3. There is atmosphere to protect us _____ the sun's deadly rays.
4. The food of the plant is different _____ that of animals.
5. Washing food down with water as a substitute _____ chewing is not a good idea.
6. He always turned on the lights _____ a random order.
7. The first group remembered 80 percent of the words, compared _____ 30 percent of the words for the second group.
8. Chunking consists _____ grouping separate bits of information.
9. That part of the moon facing away _____ the sun appears dark.
10. You have to put up _____ the advertising if you want the entertainment.
11. This case is not as easy as I thought _____ first.
12. She was not well prepared _____ too much new technology in the office all at once.
13. She showed particular interest _____ many things which other people failed to see.
14. Have you seen my door key in the kitchen _____ any chance?
15. They are not satisfied _____ the conclusion they have come to.
16. _____ contrast, the modern husband may do some of the household jobs, and it is not unusual _____ him to cook.
17. Our first acquaintance _____ these words comes from books that we read.
18. The popular words belong _____ the people _____ and large are not the possession of a limited class.

19. His answer _____ the questions were not correct, but _____ least he bagan to seek some explanations.

20. Problems arise _____ a variety of ways, and some may simply result _____ reading and thinking.

II. Choose the correct answer

1. He will be through with his work _____ half an hour.
   A. in   B. after   C. for   D. during

2. He came early and sat _____ the class in order to hear the speaker clearly.
   A. in the front of   B. in front of   C. before   D. ahead of

3. Some articles have arisen in price _____ the increasing costs.
   A. since   B. due to   C. but for   D. because

4. A foreign languge can be learned only _____ practice.
   A. with   B. through   C. by way   D. in

5. The hotel has made a rule _____ keeping animals in bedrooms.
   A. against   B. for   C. in   D. by

6. Mr. Jone got very sick _____ too hard.
   A. for working   B. from working   C. by working   D. to work

7. In Britain, meat is sold _____ the pound.
   A. at   B. in   C. with   D. by

8. The prizes will be distributed _____ seven winners.
   A. between   B. among   C. within   D. to

9. The theatre has been booked up _____ a few seats in the stalls.
   A. except   B. except for   C. besides   D. but

10. _____ the bad weather, the airplane was delayed.
    A. Due to   B. Because   C. For   D. Owing to

11. That soldier was wounded _____ the leg.
    A. on   B. in   C. at   D. under

12. I sympathize with the Women's Liberation Movement only _____ a certain extent.
    A. at   B. to   C. with   D. in

13. We are accustomed _____ late on weekends.
    A. for sleeping   B. to sleep   C. to sleeping   D. at sleeping

14. The prisoners' request _____ more and better food is now _____ consideration.
    A. to—on   B. for—under   C. of—in   D. for—into

15. We must take every caution _____ accidents.
    A. to   B. with   C. against   D. in

16. Mr. Smith is an engineer _____ profession.
    A. by   B. in   C. for   D. on

17. This boy is particularly weak _____ mathematics.
    A. out				B. at				C. with			D. from
18. I have given you my advice. Whether you will act on it is _____ you.
    A. up to			B. up for			C. on to		D. for to
19. He tried to make up _____ the lost time _____ staying up late.
    A. with—with		B. with—by			C. for—with		D. for—by
20. Before leaving the country, the young couple sold their house _____ six thousand dollars.
    A. at				B. for				C. with			D. on

Unit 19　形容词和副词的基本用法 (Basics of Adjectives and Adverbs)

导入 (Lead-in)

That's a *wise* decision.
那是明智的决定。
We treasure our *cultural* heritage.
我们珍视我们的文化遗产。
Their idea was *absolute* independent.
他们的理想是完全独立的。
The lady seemed *distressed*.
那位夫人显得很痛苦。
Statistics on juvenile delinquency are *alarming*.
少年犯罪的统计数字令人惊讶。
Have you heard anything *interesting* lately?
你最近有没有听到过有趣的事?

He is *undoubtedly* the greatest musician of the country.
他毫无疑问是这个国家最伟大的音乐家。
Obviously, he is an ideal teacher.
很明显,他是位理想的教师。
The ship sank *quickly* rather than *slowly*.
船沉得很快,而非很慢。
The old worker is *highly* respected by the young men.
这位老工人受到年轻人的尊重。
She died in an accident *shortly* afterwards.
她在不久以后的一次事故中死了。

斜体部分的词是什么词?它们跟它们所修饰的部分有什么关系,位置如何?

讲解 (Explanation)

> 形容词(Adjectives)是用来修饰名词、代词,表示其属性的词

● 形容词的用法

an **interesting** story 有趣的故事
something **important** 重要的事
anything **wrong** 错误的事
President Abraham Lincoln was a **self-made** man.
林肯总统是一个自学成才的人。

> 形容词在句中的位置如何?起什么作用?

> 形容词作定语修饰名词时,一般要放在名词的前边。但是如果形容词修饰不定代词时(由 one, no, any, some, every 构成的复合词),要放在这些词之后。

Most leaders were **well-educated**.
大多数领导都受过良好的教育。

> 形容词作表语放在系动词后,主要的系动词有:be, become, get, prove, turn, look, sound, feel, taste, smell。

Do sit down and make yourself **comfortable**.
请坐,不要拘束。

> 形容词作宾语补足语一般放在宾语的后面,对宾语进行补充说明。

She arrived home, **hungry and tired**.
她回到家,又饿又累。

> 形容词作状语位于句首或句末,相当于省略形式的状语从句,表原因或者方式。

The current fair, **the biggest in its history**, is being held in Shanghai.
有史以来规模最大的一届展销会正在上海举行。

> 形容词作同位语或者独立成分可以放在句首或句末。

☞ 思考:动词的现在分词和过去分词放在名词前,它们的作用是否相当于形容词?现在分词和过去分词修饰名词有什么区别?

> 副词(Adverb)是用来修饰动词、形容词、副词或全句的词，说明时间、地点、程度、方式等概念。

● 副词的用法

> 副词在句子中的位置如何？有什么作用？

Mary is a **very** bright girl.
玛丽是个非常聪明的女孩。(very 作状语修饰形容词 bright)
You can speak English **quite** well.
你的英语说的很好。(quite 作状语修饰副词 well)

> 作状语(主要用来修饰动词、形容词和副词)。

☞ 思考：句中的副词用来修饰句子的什么成分？

They will be **back** in five days' time.
他们五天后回来。
How long have you been **here**?
你在这儿待多久了？

> 作表语。

The desk there is not high **enough**.
那边的椅子不够高。
On our way home, I came across an old friend of **mine**.
在我们回家的路上，我遇到了一位老朋友。

> 作定语(一般放在所修饰词的后面)。

重点及难点 (Key points)

● 以 结尾的形容词

大部分形容词加 ly 构成副词，但是 friendly, deadly(致命的), lovely, lonely(孤独的), likely(可能的), lively, ugly(丑陋的), brotherly(兄弟般的), motherly(母亲般的), fatherly(父亲般的), costly(昂贵的)等仍为形容词。

Unit 19　形容词和副词的基本用法

● 多个形容词修饰名词的顺序

一般的排列顺序是：指示代词（物主代词、冠词）+ 数词 + 形状 + 性质 + 颜色 + 新旧长幼 + 原材料 + 名词

如：
a **beautiful little yellow** flower 一朵漂亮的黄色小花
a **short young Japanese** businessman 一位身材矮小的年轻日本商人
an **old stone** bridge 一座老石桥

● 形容词与副词辨析

有些副词后面加上 -ly 以后，仍为副词，但意思有所变化。

close 与 closely

close 意思是"近"；closely 意思是"仔细地"。
He is sitting **close** to me.
他就坐在我身边。
Watch him **closely**.
盯着他。

late 与 lately 的区别

late 的意思是"晚"；lately 意思是"最近"。
You have come too **late**.
你来得太晚了。
What have you been doing **lately**?
近来好吗？

deep 与 deeply 的区别

deep 意思是"深"，表示空间深度；deeply 表示抽象的深度。
He pushed the stick **deep** into the mud.
他把棍子深深插进泥里。
Even father was **deeply** moved by the film.
老爸也被电影深深打动了。

high 与 highly 的区别

high 表示空间高度，highly 表示程度，相当于 much。
The plane was flying **high**.
这架飞机飞得很高。
I think **highly** of your opinion.
你的看法很有道理。

163

wide 与 widely 的区别

wide 表示空间宽度，widely 意思是"广泛地"，"在许多地方"。

He opened the door **wide**.
他把门开得大大的。
English is **widely** used in the world.
英语在世界范围内广泛使用。

free 与 freely 的区别

free 的意思是"免费"，freely 的意思是"无限制地。"

You can eat **free** in my restaurant whenever you like.
无论什么时候，我这饭店都对你免费开放。
You can speak **freely**; say what you like.
你可以畅所欲言，想说什么就说什么。

应用 (Practice)

1. One car went too fast and _____ missed hitting another car.
   A. completely   B. greatly   C. narrowly   D. little
2. The picture was bought at a very low price, but it has turned out to be a(n) _____ painting.
   A. invaluable   B. invariable   C. worthless   D. valueless
3. Eating an apple a day is considered _____.
   A. healthy   B. healthful   C. healthily   D. health
4. As a writer, Walter was very _____.
   A. imaginary   B. imaginable   C. imaginative   D. imagery
5. I was _____ when I learnt that your application for the post of secretary had been unsuccessful.
   A. regrettable   B. regretted   C. regretful   D. regrettably
6. The book is not _____ what we paid.
   A. worth   B. valuable   C. worthy   D. expensive
7. The modern machine proved _____ in heart surgery.
   A. high valuable   B. highly valuable   C. valuable high   D. valuable highly
8. They _____ thought that the truth would be finally discovered.
   A. little   B. not   C. small   D. bit
9. They hardly believe that the apartment which costs them $ 4,000 is _____.
   A. so small   B. such little   C. so little   D. such small
10. If a claim is kept _____, it is more likely to be recognized.
    A. live   B. lived   C. alive   D. living

11. On his way to school he met a _____, so he sent him to hospital.
    A. very ill man   B. much sick man   C. serious ill man   D. very sick man
12. She was operated on a month ago and now she was _____.
    A. very good   B. very well   C. healthy   D. good conditioned
13. What I would do is to go _____.
    A. really quietly somewhere   B. somewhere quietly really
    C. really quiet somewhere   D. somewhere really quiet
14. The chairman asked _____ to write their questions on a piece of paper and send them to the front.
    A. the present members   B. the members presently
    C. the members present   D. the presently members
15. The trousers are _____, but Tom does not care a bit.
    A. too a little small   B. a little too small
    C. a too little small   D. a small too little
16. Kasia is taking her _____ tour of the shops in search of bargains.
    A. daily   B. day   C. day time   D. night
17. Although the medicine tastes _____, it seems to help my condition.
    A. bad   B. badly   C. too much bad   D. too badly
18. When she got her first month salary, Diana bought herself _____ dress.
    A. a cotton, blue, expensive   B. an expensive, blue, cotton
    C. a blue, expensive, cotton   D. a cotton, expensive, blue
19. The doctors have tried _____ to save the life of the wounded soldier.
    A. everything possible humanly   B. humanly everything possible
    C. everything humanly possible   D. humanly possible everything
20. I was worried very much because I'll miss my flight if the bus arrives _____.
    A. lately   B. late   C. latter   D. more later

Unit 20　形容词和副词的原级、比较级和最高级比较
(Comparison of Adjectives and Adverbs)

导入 (Lead-in)

斜体部分的词是什么词？它们跟它们所修饰的词有什么关系？

As I spoke to him he became *less and less* angry.
我对他说话的同时，他变得越来越不生气。

The chief reason for the population growth isn't *so* much a rise in birth rates *as* a fall in death rates as a result of improvements in medical care.
人口增长的主要原因与其说是出生率的提高，还不如说是因为医疗的进步而带来的死亡率下降的结果。

We are taught that a business letter should be written in a formal style *rather than* a personal style.
我们被告知商务信件应该写得比较正式而不是非常随便。

讲解 (Explanation)

 原级比较

He is **as** busy **as** before.
他和过去一样忙碌。

We will give you **as** much help **as** we can.
我们将尽量帮助你。

166

The book is not **so/as** interesting **as** I expected.
这本书没有我预想的那么有意思。
He didn't make **so/as** much progress **as** he had expected.
他没有取得他所预料的那么大的进步。
She didn't sing **so** well last night **as** she usually does.
她昨天晚上唱的没有平常好。

> 表示双方程度相等使用 as + 原级 + as 结构;
> 表示双方程度不相等使用 not so /as + 原级 +as
> as ...as 之间一定使用形容词和副词的原级,不能使用比较级和最高级。

> 用表示倍数的词或其他程度副词作修饰语时,要放在 as 结构的前面。

This room is *twice* **as** big **as** that one.
这间房间是那间房间的两倍大。

● 比较级比较

She has **better** memories **than** I.
她比我的记忆力要好。
She arrived **earlier than** the others.
她比别人早到。

> 两个事物比较,表示一个比另一个"更……",使用"比较级 + than"的结构。

The new method is **much more** *efficient* **than** the old one.
新方法比老方法效率高的多。
The situation is **far more** *complicated* **than** you could imagine.
情况比你想象的要复杂得多。

> 比较级可用 much, far, a lot, a great deal, a little, a bit 等词修饰,表示"……得多,""稍微……"的意义。

In fact, **the busier** he is, **the happier** he feels.
事实上他越忙越高兴。
The harder you work, **the more** you will learn.
你越努力学的就越多。

> 用"the+ 比较级, the + 比较级"表示"越……就越……"。

☞ 思考:是否所有的比较级比较都需要使用 than?

● 最高级比较

Autumn is **the best** season in Beijing.
秋天是北京最好的季节。
As far as I know, Tom works perhaps **the hardest** in his class.
就我所知,汤姆也许是班上学习最努力的。

> 三个或三个以上的事物比较用"the+ 最高级"结构

☞ 思考:是否英语中只有上述比较方法,有无例外呢?

 重点及难点 (Key points)

● 以 -ior 结尾的形容词的用法

这类本身具有比较意义的形容词后接介词 **to**,不能接 than,常见的词有 senior(年长的),junior(年幼的),superior(比……好的),inferior(比……差的),prior(提前的)
This engine is *superior* in many respects **to** that one.
这台发动机在许多方面优于那一台。
He is two years *senior* **to** me.
他比我大两岁。
I called on him *prior* **to** my departure.
出发前我去看过他。

● 比较级的特殊用法

> more A than B 含义相当与"与其说是 B,不如说是 A"。

He is **more** a teacher **than** a student.
与其说他是个学生不如说他是个老师。

> other than 不同于……, 非……。

Unit 20 形容词和副词的原级、比较级和最高级比较

The truth is quite **other than** what you think.
实际情况远非你想的那样。

> 比较级前可以用定冠词,表示"两者中较……的一个"。

She is **the taller** of the two sisters.
她是两姐妹中较高的一个。

> 避免将主语含在比较对象中。

China is **larger than any** country in Asia. (×)
中国比亚洲任何一个国家都大。(中国也是亚洲国家,不能比自己大)
China is **larger than any other** country in Asia. (√)
中国比亚洲其他(不包括中国)任何国家都大。

The polulation of Shanghai is **larger than** Beijing. (×)
上海的人口比北京多。(上海的人口不能和北京比较,只能和北京的人口比较)
The population of Shanghai is **larger than** that of beijing. (√)
上海的人口比北京(的人口)多。

应用 (Practice)

Choose the correct answer

1. This new instrument is far superior _____ the old one we bought three years ago.
   A. than　　　　B. to　　　　C. over　　　　D. of
2. They are _____ students that they all performed well in the nationwide examinations.
   A. so diligent　　B. such diligent　　C. so much diligent　　D. such very diligent
3. My new glasses cost me _____ the last pair that I bought.
   A. three times　　　　　　　　B. three times as much as
   C. three times as much　　　　D. three times much as
4. They spent all their spare time, _____ their spare money, on their experiments.
   A. as much as　　B. as well as　　C. as long as　　D. as soon as
5. The experiment was _____ easier than we had expected.
   A. more　　　　B. much more　　C. much　　　　D. more much

169

6. She is older than _____.
   A. any other girl in the group   B. any girl in the group
   C. all girls in the group   D. you and me as well as the group
7. My _____ brother is six years _____ than I am. He is _____ of the three brother.
   A. older, older, oldest   B. elder, elder, eldest
   C. older, older, the oldest   D. elder, older, the eldest
8. Jack is _____ more intelligent than his brother.
   A. very   B. so   C. greatly   D. far
9. "Ralph seems to like this country."
   "Yes, he is _____ here as he was at home."
   A. almost as happy   B. almost happy as   C. as almost happy   D. as happy almost
10. Ships can carry _____ goods than any other means of transport.
   A. many   B. much   C. more   D. better
11. A child is not so free to do as he wishes _____ he thinks older people are.
   A. as   B. than   C. that   D. so
12. In some modern countries we find a _____ number of people with university degrees than there are jobs for them to fill.
   A. large   B. far larger   C. more large   D. more larger
13. Now that I am working for my living, I do not have _____ time as before to spend on my stamps.
   A. much   B. more   C. as much   D. more than
14. It is not so _____ it appears to introduce equal pay for equal work.
   A. easy   B. easier than C. easier as   D. easy as
15. It seems reasonable that the younger and therefore less experienced worker gets _____ than the older and more experienced one.
   A. less   B. more   C. as much   D. so much
16. Summer is _____ part of the year, and at the same time we are the busiest in the town.
   A. hot   B. hotter   C. a hottest   D. the hottest
17. The more we get togethr, _____ we shall be.
   A. the happy   B. happier   C. the happier   D. the more happy
18. This case is not as _____ as I thought at first.
   A. easy   B. easier   C. more easy   D. more easier
19. One of _____ mountain ranges of the world rises from the Atlantic.
   A. the largest   B. the most large   C. the larger   D. the much largest

Unit 21　不定代词
(Indefinite Pronouns)

 导入 (Lead-in)

下面代词有什么不同，什么叫做不定代词？

my, their, yourself, who, whose, he, it, these, mine
some, all, both, something, little, either, another

看看下面的句子，想想斜体部分的词在句子中起什么作用。

There are trees and flowers at *each* side of the road.
路边都是树木和鲜花。

The medicine is on sale everywhere. You can get it at *any* chemist's.
这种药到处都出售。你可以在任何药店买到它。

They were all tired, but *none* of them would stop to have a rest.
他们都累了，但是没有人停下来休息。

No agreement was reached in the discission as *neither* side would give way to the other.
任何一方都不愿意向对方让步，所以讨论没能达成最后的任何一致。

讲解 (Explanation)

> 不定代词是用来指代非特定对象,代替名词或形容词,表示各种程度和不定数量的词。

● **one 和 ones 的用法**

One should always try to help others.
所有的人／任何人都应当试着帮助别人。
One should never lose heart in face of difficulties.
在困难面前,人决不应该灰心丧气。
The coat is too small for me. I want a bigger **one**.
这件衣服我穿太小了,我想要件大点的。
The books here are easy but the **ones** there are rather difficult.
这儿的书简单,但是那儿的书很难。

> one 可以泛指任何人,也可以在形容词或 this, that 等词后代替刚提过的可数名词,复数形式为 ones。

☞ 思考：上面句中的 one 和 ones 各代替句中的什么成分？

● **each 和 every 的用法**

We have two copies **each**. 我们每个人有两本书。(each 作 we 的同位语)
Every dog has its day. 每个人都有得意的时候。(every 作定语修饰 dog)

> each 和 every 都表示"每个"的意思,但 each 强调个别,可以充当主语、宾语、定语和同位语。every 强调整体,相当于"每个都",在句中只作定语。

Each of the two has won a prize. 他们俩每个人都获奖了。(两个人)
Every student in our class likes English. 我们班每个同学都喜欢英语。(三人以上)

> each 所代表的数可以是两个或两个以上,而 every 所指的数必须是三个以上。

every two days = **every** other day = **every** second day 每两天(每隔一天)
every other line 每隔一行

> every 可与基数词、序数词, other, few 等连用, 表示时间或空间的间隔, 而 each 不可以。

☞ 思考: 前面几个句中 each 与 every 在句中各充当什么成分?

● one, no one 和 none 的用法

"Did **anyone** come to see me?" "有人来看我吗?"
"**No one**." 没有。(泛指人, 不强调范围, 不能用 none)
"Did **any** of my friends come to see me?" "我的朋友们有人来看我吗?"
"**None** (of them came)." "没有"。(指人, 有具体范围, 不能用 no one)
You said the books were on the table, but there were **none** there. 你说书在桌子上, 但是那儿一本书都没有。(指物, 有具体范围, 不能用 nothing 或 no one.)

> no one 是用于泛指的代词, 不强调范围, 只能指人, 相当于 nobody, 不和介词 of 构成短语。None 既可指人也可指物, 使用 none 时, 有一定的范围, 这个范围可用介词 of 构成的短语来表示, 也可以不表示出来。

 重点及难点 (Key points)

● other, others, the other, the others 和 another 的用法

> other + 名词(复数或不可数), 但如果前面有 the, this, some, any 等表示单数概念的词, 可与单数名词连用。

We should often think of **other** people.
我们应该经常考虑到他人。
The weather in Hei Longjiang is colder than that of **any other** province of China.
黑龙江的天气比中国任何其他省份都冷。

> others = other + 名词, 泛指"别的人或物"(但不是全部)。

Some planted trees; **others** watered them.
一些人种树, 其他人(并非全部)在浇水。

> the other 指"两者中的另外一个",常用结构是:one... the other...

He has two brothers. One is a doctor. The other is a teacher.
他有两个哥哥。一位是医生,另一位是教师。

> another 表示"又一……"、"再一……",一般用来代替或修饰可数的单数词,前面不加冠词。

Could I have another cup of tea?
我能再喝一杯茶吗?

☞ 思考:other, the other, another 后面是否要有被修饰的词,others, the others 后面一定不加被修饰的词吗?

● some 和 any 的用法

> some(一些)和 any(任何一个)可以修饰可数名词和不可数名词。some 和 any 都可以作代词。some 一般用于肯定句,any 多用于否定句、疑问句和条件句中。

Some enjoy playing basketball. Some like football.
一些人喜欢篮球,一些人喜欢足球。
I have some English books but I haven't any French ones.
我有一些英语书,但没有法语书。
Any book will do.
任何一本书都可以。
Have any of you actually seen a UFO?
你们中间是不是有人确实看到过飞碟?

> some 可以用在肯定句中,表示希望得到肯定回答

Would you like some coffee?
你想要些咖啡吗?

> any 也可用在肯定句中,表示"任何的",相当于 every

He is taller than any other boy in the class.
他比班上其他任何男孩都高。

You can get it from any student.
你可以从任何一个学生那里获得。

> some 作"某一"，与单数可数名词连用。

Some person is waiting for you at the gate.
有个人在大门口等你。

● it, one 和 that 的用法

> it 可指代可数名词和不可数名词。常常指代上文中"the+ 名词"或"物主代词 + 名词"中的名词，表示同一件事物，但 it 代替的事物属于特指。他的复数是 they 或 them。

The Parkers bought a new house but it will need a lot of work before they can move in.
帕克一家买了一栋新房子，但是他们搬进来之前还有许多工作需要做。

> one 所表示的名词（可指人或物）和前面所提到的名词只是同一类的任何一个，不是指其中某一个。不可代替不可数名词。复数形式是 ones。

I hope there are enough glasses for each guest to have one.
我希望有足够的玻璃杯，每位客人能有一个。

> That 代表的也是同一类事物而不是同一事物，但 that 代替的是有冠词的名词，表特指，也还可以代替不可数名词。用 that 来代替前面已出现的可数名词或不可数名词时，后面一定要跟修饰语，且 that 只能指物。

No bread eaten by man is sweet as that earned by his own labor.
享受自己的劳动果实是最甜美的事情。

应用 (Practice)

1. He asked me for _____ ink, but I hadn't _____.
   A. some, some   B. a few, any   C. some, any   D. any, some
2. One of the two women in the room is my aunt, and _____ is a friend of _____.
   A. the other, hers   B. another, her   C. other, her   D. other, hers
3. I don't like the color of the coat. Show me _____, please.
   A. another   B. the others   C. other   D. another one

4. My mother bought me two hats, but I like _____ of them.
   A. both   B. either   C. none   D. neither
5. There are tall trees on _____ of the river.
   A. every side   B. both side   C. either side   D. all sides
6. They were all asleep. _____ of them heard the sound.
   A. None   B. No one   C. All   D. Not everyone
7. Mary and John have arrived, but _____ students aren't here yet.
   A. other   B. the other   C. the others   D. others
8. They got on well and learned from _____.
   A. each other   B. one to another C. one after another D. one and another
9. "Is _____ here?"
   "No, Bob and Tim have asked for leave."
   A. anybody   B. somebody   C. everybody   D. nobody
10. Can you believe that in _____ a rich country there should be _____ many poor people?
    A. such, such   B. such, so   C. so, so   D. so, such
11. "When shall we meet again?"
    "Make _____ day you like; it's all the same to me."
    A. one   B. any   C. another   D. some
12. Few pleasures can equal _____ of a cool drink on a hot day.
    A. some   B. any   C. that   D. those
13. The amount of money spent on cosmetics, according o some authorities, has exceeded _____ spent on public health.
    A. one   B. those   C. it   D. that

其他类型

I. In this section, there are 10 incomplete sentences. You are required to complete each one by deciding on the most appropriate word or words from the 4 choices marked A, B, C and D.

1. It was not until yesterday evening _____ the manager made his decision known.
   A. when   B. that   C. as   D. so

2. It was because I wanted to buy a dictionary _____ I went downtown yesterday.
   A. but   B. and   C. why   D. that

3. It was in China _____ the agreement was signed.
   A. that   B. which   C. where   D. what

4. Seldom _____ my boss in such good mood since I came to work in this company.
   A. I saw   B. I have been   C. have I seen D. do I see

5. Little _____ that the police are about to arrest him.
   A. he knows   B. he doesn't know   C. does he know   D. doesn't he know

6. So loudly _____ that the audience in the back heard him clearly.
   A. does he speak B. did he speak C. he speaks   D. he spoke

7. It was in that small village _____ our president was born.
   A. which   B. when   C. that   D. as

8. Since Dick was busy, he rarely had time to go the cinema, _____.
   A. Jane did too B. Jane didn't as well   C. so did Jane   D. nor did Jane

9. He is used to flying by air and on no occasion _____ frightened.
   A. he has ever felt   B. he ever feels
   C. ever does he feel   D. has he ever felt

10. So _____ after she learned the good news that she could hardly fall asleep that night.
    A. excited the mother was   B. was the mother excited
    C. the mother was excited   D. excited was the mother

11. So loudly _____ that people could hear it out in the street.
    A. did the students play the music   B. the students playing the music
    C. the students played the music   D. have the students played the music

12. Not for a moment _____ the truth of your explanation about the event.
    A. we have doubted   B. did we doubt   C. we had doubted   D. doubted we

13. Not until quite recently _____ any idea of what a guided rocket is like.

            A. did I have   B. do I have   C. should I have   D. would I have
    14. He told me that I _____ be present at the ceremony.
            A. could   B. would   C. should   D. might
    15. Either of the children _____ quite capable of looking after the baby.
            A. are   B. be   C. is   D. have been
    16. The weather report says that there will be a storm _____ two days.
            A. until   B. before   C. in   D. by
    17. _____ his surprise, the manager found nobody in the meeting room.
            A. At   B. To   C. For   D. With
    18. The Accident was my fault, so I had to pay for the damage _____ the other car.
            A. at   B. to   C. on   D. for
    19. Try not to be absent _____ class again for the rest of the term.
            A. from   B. on   C. in   D. of
    20. My boss said that he was badly _____ need of my assistance.
            A. at   B. in   C. for   D. with
    21. The chair looks rather unusual in shape, but it is very comfortable to sit _____.
            A. by   B. on   C. with   D. at
    22. If you are worried _____ the problem, you should do something about it.
            A. with   B. for   C. on   D. about
    23. Mary is the kind of person who always seems to be _____ a hurry.
            A. on   B. in   C. with   D. for
    24. I think Anna is _____ far the most active member in our group.
            A. with   B. at   C. as   D. by
    25. Our president will hold a special party at May Flower Hotel tonight _____ your honor.
            A. with   B. at   C. in   D. on
    26. I haven't met him _____ the last committee meeting.
            A. for   B. since   C. at   D. before
    27. This company has two branches: one in Paris and _____ in New York.
            A. another   B. one other   C. the other   D. other
    28. We don't deny that your products are superior in quality to _____ of Japanese make.
            A. the one   B. that   C. these   D. those
    29. We've got two TV sets, but we still can't watch anything because _____ works properly.
            A. each   B. either   C. neither   D. every
    30. The grain output of this year is much higher than _____ of last year.
            A. that   B. such   C. which   D. what
    31. All my classmates have passed the physical education exam except _____.

     A. John and I   B. John and me   C. I and John   D. me and John

32. Tom _____ the party as no one saw him there yesterday evening.
    A. can't attend   B. mustn't attend
    C. won't have attended   D. couldn't have attended

33. His mother told me that he _____ read quite well at the age of five.
    A. should   B. would   C. could   D. might

34. I am going to attend the conference, but you _____ with me.
    A. needn't to go   B. don't need go   C. needn't go   D. needn't going

II. There are 10 incomplete statements here. You should fill in each blank with the proper form of the word given in the brackets.

1. The little child dare not (walk) _____ in the forest alone.
2. The policemen (tell) _____ not to take any action until they received further order.
3. The father wants to know why his son (question) _____ by the police last week.
4. Dr. Richard, together with his wife and three children, (be) _____ to arrive in Beijing this afternoon.
5. Neither the clerks nor the manager (know) _____ anything about the accident now.
6. Both of the twin brothers (be) _____ capable of doing technical at present.
7. The piece of music was composed by a very famous blind (music) _____.
8. Ms. Davis is proud of her students because they are not only (hard-work) _____, but also very creative.
9. The project was not actually realized as it was not very (practice) _____.
10. The Chairman of the Board explained his point again so that there would be no (understanding) _____.
11. The manager was (entire) _____ unaware of the trouble with the heating system in the hotel until this week.
12. I'm afraid there is not much (differ) _____ in their points of view.
13. I am sure the secretary who has just been hired will prove to be an efficient (employ) _____.
14. I've heard that the musical group will set off for Hong Kong to give a three-day (perform) _____.
15. After the flood, life was (extreme) _____ difficult for the farmers in this area.
16. Before the flight takes off, all passengers are asked to (fast) _____ their seat belts.
17. I cannot go shopping with you because I have an (appoint) _____ with my dentist this afternoon.
18. Following the (settle) _____ of the strike, the train service is now back to normal.
19. We should read more and see more in order to (wide) _____ our horizons.
20. Some experts suggest that we slow down the (economy) _____ growth in the country.
21. Doing a second job to earn more money also means you have to pay (addition) _____ income tax.

22. It is (reason) _____ for parents to pay for their children's education.
23. At the meeting a (propose) _____ was put forward by John Smith.
24. It has been a long winter, and we're (eager) _____ waiting for the coming of the spring.
25. They fully recognized the enormous (strong) _____ and influence of the union.
26. We are not short of raw materials at the moment, but we need reliable (equip) _____.
27. Following the (success) _____ settlement of the strike, the train service is now back to normal.
28. With his knowledge and experience, he is no doubt (qualify) _____ for the task.
29. If a business wants to sell its products (international) _____, it should do some world market research first.
30. My sister has recently got a job as a (reception) _____ in a hotel.
31. Provided that there is no (object) _____, we will begin with the next item.
32. There has not been a favorable (respond) _____ to your plan so far.
33. Buying a house in such a neighborhood can be a (cost) _____ business.
34. The businessman lost a (gold) _____ chance to make a big fortune.
35. You should be aware that this rare bird was on the list of human (protect) _____.
36. Did you get the (permit) _____ from the authorities to run the business?
37. They decided not to visit the Great Wall because it was raining (heavy) _____.
38. Miss Cherry is a well-known singer. She showed (music) _____ tendencies from her early age.
39. Yesterday I was late getting to the railway station, but (fortunate) _____, the train was late, too.
40. The bank became suspicious after several large (withdraw) _____ were made from his account in a single week.
41. The young man made several constructive suggestions about the environmental (protect) _____ in this city.
42. The local government is trying to raise money to (modern) _____ the city's public transport systems.
43. Her early (arrive) _____ gave everyone a big surprise.
44. A meal containing fish and vegetables is considered a (health) _____ one.
45. After careful (consider) _____, the committee agreed on the proposal.
46. The little girl gave an (extreme) _____ wonderful performance last night.
47. That street is a very (desire) _____ place for you to open a new store.
48. This is a very (danger) _____ road: there were at least five serious accidents last year.
49. We've never had any problem with our car in the past three years; it's highly reliable in (operate) _____.
50. The place was so (attract) _____ that the tourists spent much more time there than in any other place.

51. The local people are very (friend) _____ to the visiting tourists.
52. Going abroad to have a holiday will be an (excite) _____ experience for us.
53. Some people do believe that smoking will (certain) _____ cause lung cancer.
54. With the (develop) _____ of foreign trade, more and more people are doing import and export business.
55. It was very (help) _____ of you to make all the necessary arrangements for us.
56. On hearing the good news that our new products sold well in the market, we all got (excite) _____.
57. Living in the country is less (expense) _____ than living in the city.
58. He is asked to (short) _____ his report to one page.
59. His suggestion turned out to be very (effect) _____ in the improvement of our production.
60. It is difficult for a (foreign) _____ to learn Chinese.
61. She is well-known for her excellent (achieve) _____ in her career.
62. He is (confidence) _____ even though he has failed several times.
63. I have decided to accept their (invite) _____ to pay a visit to their factory.
64. He seemed very young, but he was (real) _____ older than all of us.
65. John's performance in this exam made us feel rather (disappoint) _____.
66. It was (luck) _____ indeed for Mr. Fox to have changed his flight and arrived safe.
67. To his mother's relief, Tom had perfectly recovered from his _____ (ill).
68. I'm afraid my attempt to make a cake wasn't very (success) _____.
69. In the museum, foreign visitors are especially interested in that ancient (paint) _____.
70. The secretary is so efficient that his boss think (high) _____ of him.
71. She was not happy because he had kept her (wait) _____ for half an hour.
72. Mary told me not to worry because the (operate) _____ on Mr. Smith was very successful.
73. His wife was sure that he would arrive on time. This (certain) _____ made her rush to prepare the dinner.
74. The (manage) _____ of a company is a very important part of the working process to its development.
75. Although John was not experienced in business, he did it with (confident) _____.
76. I'm (real) _____ sorry for the mistake our office worker made in the business last month.
77. Your ideas are very interesting, but we need some (practice) _____ advice for getting out of the trouble.
78. The manager has received only one (apply) _____ for the post.
79. Don't you think their rents (reason) _____?
80. Mary had made up her mind to go and what I said to her didn't make any (different) _____.

81. I thought this explanation was (unnecessary) _____ complex.
82. The boss has promised a wage increase for all the (employ) _____.
83. The sellers allowed us to pay them on a (month) _____ basis.
84. I didn't attend the evening party; but (apparent) _____, it was a great success.
85. The chairman emphasized his ideas by speaking more (loud) _____.
86. There has been a large (grow) _____ of light industries during these years.
87. The manager asked the secretary to (short) _____ the report to 600 words.

附录一　自然拼读法 (Phonics)

是 26 个英语字母不同的排列组合。自然拼读法学习的就是这 26 个字母的发音规则,掌握了自然拼读法,就掌握了英语字母和语音的对应关系,有利于读单词和记忆单词。

I. 掌握 26 个字母的读音

> 1. 5 个元音字母(a, e, i, o, u),每个发两种音:字母本身音和短音。在 c**a**t, b**e**d, b**i**g, d**o**g, c**u**p 这五个单词里,a, e, i, o, u 发的是短音。
> 2. 21 个辅音字母发音大多与字母读音对应,注意 x 发 /ks/。
> 3. y 不在单词开头时,被看成是元音。

II. 单元音单词拼读

> 如果一个英语单词或音节里只有一个元音,且元音不在末尾,这个元音一般发短音。

如：h**a**t, m**a**p, b**a**t, c**a**p, l**a**p, m**a**n, h**a**nd, b**a**n
　　g**e**t, b**e**t, b**e**d, l**e**t, n**e**t, l**e**nd, t**e**n, f**e**d
　　s**i**t, b**i**t, b**i**g, l**i**p, h**i**t, h**i**s, h**i**m, d**i**p
　　b**o**ss, d**o**t, g**o**t, d**o**g, f**o**g, fr**o**g, l**o**t, n**o**d
　　b**u**t, b**u**g, c**u**p, c**u**t, m**u**g, n**u**t, d**u**ck, h**u**t

III. 双元音单词拼读

> 如果一个英语单词或音节里有两个元音,则前一个元音发其字母本身音,而后一个元音不发音。

如：c**a**ke, d**a**te, k**i**te, d**i**ne, h**o**le, n**o**te, m**u**te, h**u**ge
　　m**a**y, m**a**il, d**ee**r, m**ea**l, d**ie**, t**oe**, k**e**y, b**oa**t, r**oa**d

IV. 元音在末尾

> 如果一个单词或音节里只有一个元音,且元音在末尾,那么这个元音一般发字母本身音。

如:t**a**ble, m**e**, h**e**, h**i**, s**i**lence, g**o**, n**o**, h**u**man, t**u**mor

> y 在单音节词尾时,发 i 的字母本身音,在多音节词尾时,发 e 的字母本身音。

如:m**y**, b**y**, fl**y**, sk**y**, wh**y**, dr**y**, tr**y**
bab**y**, momm**y**, dadd**y**, wind**y**, cloud**y**

V. 辅音联读

> 两个或三个辅音在一起时要联读。

如:**bl**ack, **pl**ease, **fr**ee, **br**ead, **str**eet, **spl**it, **dr**ive, **cl**ap, **sm**art
li**ft**, **sw**amp, la**nd**, ba**nk**, beast, ri**sk**

> 记住 ch, sh, th, wh 的读法。

如:**ch**eese, **ch**ip, bea**ch**, ben**ch**
sheep, **sh**irt, fi**sh**, pu**sh**
three, **th**ank, bo**th**, grow**th**
they, **th**ose, wi**th**
thite, **th**at, **th**ich, **th**y

VI. 带元音的特殊读法

> 有些元音和辅音组合在一起,成为整体音节。

如: ar   c**ar**, f**ar**, m**ar**ch, b**ar**
    air   h**air**, ch**air**
    al   **al**l, h**al**l, t**al**k, w**al**k
    alt   s**alt**, h**alt**
    are   h**are**, m**are**, b**are**
    au   c**au**tion, p**au**se, cl**au**se
    aught c**aught**, t**aught**, n**aught**y
    aw   h**aw**k, dr**aw**, p**aw**

ay	day, may, bay, clay	
eigh	eight, weight, sleigh	
ew	new, few, hew	
ed	发 /ed/	added, lifted, invited
	发 /t/	hoped, stopped, talked
	发 /d/	failed, cried, played
er	teacher, sister, member	
ir	birth, firm, stir	
ur	fur, turn, hurt	
ie	field, wield, piece	
igh	high, light, right, night, sight	
ing	sing, king	
ind	find, kind, bind, behind	
ild	wild, mild, child	
oi	oil, soil, noise	
old	cold, bold, sold	
oo	book, cook, hook	
oo	tool, tooth, noodle, school	
ost	host, most, ghost	
or	sort, form, lord	
ou	house, loud, shout, mouse	
ought	ought, brought, sought	
ould	could, would, should	
ous	famous, nervous	
ow	cow, how, now	
ow	low, snow, blow	
oy	boy, toy, destroy	
tion	attention, relation, operation	
sion	expression, impression, passion	
ough	(有五种发音) cough, through, ought, slough, plough	

VII. 辅音的特殊读法

> 有时候有些辅音不发音。

如：b 不发音　　comb, lamb, climb
　　h 不发音　　ghost, hour, honor
　　k 不发音　　knife, know, knock
　　w 不发音　　write, wrist, wreck

> c 和 g 后面若是字母 i(或 y)或 e，则 c 发 /s/，g 发 /j/ 的音；其他情况下，c 发 /k/，g 发 /g/ 的音。

如：city, celebrate, nice, cigar, center,
　　gym, generation, giant
　　cat, cute, cold, can, care
　　gate, goat, good, grey, gun

例外：give, get

> c 和 k 在一起发 /k/ 的音。

如：duck, quick, chicken, black

> q 总是和 u 在一起。

如：quarter, quality, quit, quiet, quote

> p 和 h 在一起发 /f/ 的音。

如：photo, phase, paragraph

VIII. 多音节单词和复合词

> 有两个或两个以上音节的单词是多音节单词。
> 由两个或两个以上的词复合构成的词叫复合词。

如：(多音节) listen, impossible, interesting, standard
　　(复合词) housework, mailbox, policeman, sidewalk

附录二 词的派生法 (Derivation)

前缀：一般只改变词的意义，不改变词类

1) 用于形容词、副词或名词前表示相反的含义

    un-   unfair 不公正的   unexpected 意想不到的
    dis-   dishonest 不诚实的   discouraging 令人泄气的
    non- nonsense 废话   non-smoker 不抽烟的人
    in-   incomplete 不完整的   inexpensive 不贵的
    im-   impossible 不可能的   immoral 不道德的   （用于以 m, p 开头的词之前）
    ir-   irregular 不规则的   irresponsible 不负责的   （用于以 r 开头的词之前）
    il-   illegal 非法的   illogical 不合逻辑的 （用于以 l 开头的词之前）
invaluable 含义为"非常宝贵的、无法估计的"，并不表示否定含义。

2) 用于动词前表示相反的动作

    un- 解开   undress 使脱衣服   uncover 揭开盖子
    dis- 分离、剥夺、除去   disclose 揭露   disarm 解除武装
    de- 分离、降低   decompose 分解   devalue 使贬值

3) 用在动词前表示错误

    mis-   mistake 错误   misunderstand 误解

4) 用于名词前表示程度和大小

    super- 超级   supermodle 超级名模   supermarket 超级市场
    mini- 小，微量   minibus 小公共汽车   miniskirt 超短裙
    micro 小   microwave 微波   microscope 显微镜

5) 用于动词和名词前表示时间和顺序

    re- 再   remarry 再婚   replay 再次播放
    pre- 预先，在……前
    post- 在……后   postgraduate 研究生   postwar 战后

后缀:后缀一般只改变词性,不引起词义变化

1) 由动词构成名词,表示人或器具

-er	……的人	writer 作家	villager 村民
-or	……者	inventor 发明家	
-ist	专业人员	geologist 地理学家	communist 共产主义者
-ee	受动者	examinee 考生	employee 雇员
-er	施动者	examiner 考官	employer 雇主
-ian	精通……的人	musician 音乐家	
-an	……地方的人	Russian 俄国人	African 非洲人
-ese	……地方的人	Chinese 中国人	Japanese 日本人
-ess	表示阴性	actress 女演员	
-ant	……者	assistant 助手	accountant 会计

2) 由形容词构成名词,表示性质或者状态:

-ness	kindness 善意	happiness 快乐
-ship	hardship 艰苦	friendship 友谊
-y	difficulty 困难	
-ity	reality 现实	possibility 可能性
-ty	safty 安全	anxiety 焦急
-th	wealth 富裕	warmth 温暖
-ence	difference 区别	convenience 方便
-ance	performance 表演	importance 重要性
-dom	freedom 自由	wisedom 智慧

3) 由动词构成名词,表示动作、过程或结果

-(t)ion	pollution 污染	
-ation	invitation 邀请	observation 观察
-(s)ion	discussion 讨论	impression 现象
-ing	swimming 游泳	teaching 教导
-ure	failture 失败	
-ment	development 发展	agreement 同意
-al	refusal 拒绝	approval 批准
-age	marriage 结婚	

以下几个词构成名词时词形发生变化
explain—explanation 解释   pronunce—pronunciation 发音   repeat—repetition 重复

4) 由名词构成名词表示身份、时代、资格或职位

-hood	childhood 童年	neighbourhood 附近
-ship	professorship 教授职位	citizenship 公民资格

5) 由名词或形容词构成名词表示"主义"

-ism   socialism 社会主义   communism 共产主义

6) 有名词构成形容词表示"具有……性质"或"与……有关"

-ful	useful 有用的	cheerful 高兴的
-ive	active 活跃的	imaginative 有想象力的
-ous	dangerous 危险的	
-ly	lonely 孤独的	
-al	practical 实用的	educational 教育的
-ent	excellent 优秀的	
-ant	important 重要的	
-ary	imaginary 幻想的	primary 首要的
-y	healthy 健康的	wealthy 富裕的
-some	troublesome 令人烦恼的	
-an	European 欧洲的	Canadian 加拿大的
-en	woolen 羊毛的	golden 金色的

7) 由动词等构成形容词表示"可……的"或"能……的"

-able	suitable 合适的	reliable 可靠的
-ible	impossible 不可能的	responsible 负责的

8) 由名词构成形容词表示否定意义

-less   useless 无用的   fearless 无畏的

priceless (宝贵的、无价的)   countless (无数的) 并不表示否定意义
"无价值的"应该是 valueless 或 worthless

9) 由形容词构成副词

-ly 表示方式,程度   freely 自由地   terribly 可怕地
-ward 表示方向   backward 向后   forward 向前

10) 由形容词构成动词,表示"使……化","使……成为、变得"

-ize	modernize 使现代化	industrialize 使工业化
-ify	beautify 美化	purify 净化
-en	harden 使……硬	sharpen 使……变锋利

附录三 常见词的词性转换
(Conversion of Parts of Speech)

名词	动词	形容词	副词
achievement	achieve		
addition	add	additional	additionally
		apparent	apparently
application applicant	apply		
appointment	appoint		
certainty		certain	certainly
confidence		confident	confidently
cost	cost	costly	
difference	differ	different	differently
disappointment	disappoint	disappointed disappointing	disappointedly
eagerness		eager	eagerly
economy		economic, economical	economically
effect	affect	effective	effectively
employee, employer employment	employ		
		entire	entirely
equipment	equip		
excitement	excite	excited, exciting	excitedly
expense	expend	expensive	expensively
		extreme	extremely
	fasten	fast	fast
foreigner		foreign	
friend		friendly	
gold		golden	
growth	grow		

hard-work		hardworking	
help	help	helpful	helpfully
height		high	highly
		international	internationally
invitation	invite		
illness		ill	
		loud	loudly
luck		lucky	luckily
manager, management	manage		
month		monthly	
object, objection	object		
operation	operate	operational	operationally
painting	paint		
performance	perform		
permission	permit		
practice	practice	practical	practically
proposal	propose		
protection	protect		
qualification	qualify	qualified	
reality		real	really
reason		reasonable	
reception, receptionist	receive		
settlement	settle		
	shorten	short	shortly
strength	strengthen	strong	strongly
success	succeed	successful	successfully
understanding	understand	understandable	understandably
		unnecessary	unnecessarily
width	widen	wide	widely

附录四　常见不规则动词变化
(Irregular Verbs)

不定式	过去式	过去分词
arise	arose	arisen
awake	awoke, awaked	awoken, awaked
be	was, were	been
bear	bore	borne, born
beat	beat	beaten
become	became	become
begin	began	begun
bend	bent	bent
bet	bet, betted	bet, betted
bid	bade, bid	bidden, bid
bind	bound	bound
bite	bit	bitten, bit
blend	blended, blent	blended, blent
blow	blew	blown
break	broke	broken
bring	brought	brought
broadcast	broadcast, broadcasted	broadcast, broadcasted
build	built	built
burn	burnt, burned	burnt, burned
burst	burst	burst
buy	bought	bought
cast	cast	cast
catch	caught	caught
choose	chose	chosen
come	came	come
cost	cost	cost
creep	crept	crept
cut	cut	cut

deal	dealt	dealt
dig	dug	dug
do	did	done
draw	drew	dawn
dream	dreamed, dreamt	dreamed, dreamt
drink	drank	drunk
drive	drove	driven
eat	ate	eaten
fall	fell	fallen
feed	fed	fed
feel	felt	felt
fight	fought	fought
find	found	found
fly	flew	flown
forbid	forbade	forbidden
forecast	forecast, forecasted	forecast, forecasted
forget	forgot	forgotten
forgive	forgave	forgiven
freeze	froze	frozen
get	got	gotten
give	gave	given
go	went	gone
grow	grew	grown
hang	hung hanged	hung, hanged
have	had	had
hear	heard	heard
hide	hid	hid, hidden
hit	hit	hit
hold	held	held
hurt	hurt	hurt
keep	kept	kept
know	knew	known
lay	laid	laid
lead	led	led
lean	leaned, leant	leanedm leant
leap	leapt, leaped	leapt, leaped
learn	learned, learnt	learned, learnt
leave	left	left
lend	lent	lent
let	let	let

lie	lay	lain
light	lit, lighted	lit, lighted
lose	lost	lost
make	made	made
mean	meant	meant
meet	met	met
mistake	mistook	mistaken
misunderstand	misunderstood	misunderstood
overcome	overcame	overcome
pay	paid	paid
prove	proved	proved, proven
put	put	put
quit	quit, quitted	quit, quitted
read	read	read
ride	rode	ridden
ring	rang	rung
rise	rose	risen
run	ran	run
say	saw	seen
seek	sought	sought
sell	sold	sold
send	sent	sent
set	set	set
sew	sewed	sewn, sewed
shake	shook	shaken
shave	shaved	shaved, shaven
shine	shone, shined	shone, shined
shoot	shot	shot
show	showed	shown, showed
shut	shut	shut
sing	sang	sung
sink	sank	sunk
sit	sat	sat
sleep	slept	slept
slide	slid	slid
smell	smelt, smelled	smelt, smelled
speak	spoke	spoken
speed	spoke	spoken
spell	spelt, spelled	spelt, spelled
spend	spent	spent

spill	spilt, spilled	spilt, spilled
split	split	split
spoil	spoilt, spoiled	spoilt, spoiled
spread	spread	spread
spring	sprang	sprung
stand	stood	stood
steal	stole	stolen
stick	stuck	stuck
strike	struck	struck
string	strung	strung
swear	swore	sworn
sweat	sweated, sweat	sweated, sweat
sweep	swept	swept
swim	swam	swum
swing	swung	swung
take	took	taken
teach	taught	taught
tear	tore	torn
tell	told	told
think	thought	thought
throw	threw	thrown
undergo	underwent	undergone
understand	understood	understood
undertake	undertook	undertaken
undo	undid	undone
upset	upset	upset
wake	woke, waked	woken, waked
wear	woke, waked	woken, waked
wear	wore	worn
weep	wept	wept
wet	wet, wetted	wet, wetted
win	won	won
wind	wound	wound
withdraw	withdrew	withdrawn
withstand	withstood	withstood
write	wrote	written

参考答案 (Answer Key for Reference)

Unit 1 简单句 (Simple Sentences)

II. 1. appears 2. is 3. are 4. gets 5. admit 6. is 7. have 8. have studied
9. has finished 10. is/was

III. 1. a praise 2. broken 3. the reason 4. to the chairman 5. the book 6. easier
7. respectable 8. to be tidied up / being tidied up 9. loudly
10. Without the support from his wife

Unit 2 并列句 (Compound Sentences)

II. 1. and 2. but 3. while 4. nor 5. and 6. but 7. for 8. or 9. however
10. not only... but also

III. 1. go too 2. too 3. neither do 4. doesn't either 5. so did

IV. 1. 他喜欢喝茶而他的弟弟却爱喝咖啡。
2. 他们先到了比尔家。马克受到邀请进屋喝杯可乐，看会儿电视。
3. 我找到了好几本关于这一课题的书，但这些书常常写得枯燥无味，充满学究气。
4. 我能做得更好，能够用我的幽默感及亲身经历帮助大西洋两岸的人们更加有效地进行交流，所以你要相信我。
5. 奥林匹克成功恢复，希腊宣布自己是最适合永久举办奥运会的主办国，但是顾拜旦和国际奥委会却决定要轮流举办这次体育盛会。

Unit 3 名词从句 (Noun Clauses)

I. 1. It is undoubtedly true that poverty is still a problem in this country.
2. It seems that the Americans will never stop moving.
3. We don't know how he managed to have the company sign the contract in the last.
4. I'm afraid I couldn't finish the work as you told me.
5. Maybe that's why the wives are so satisfied.
6. It is thought that the newcomer will never accept such conditions.
7. The boy didn't suppose that his father believed what he had said.
8. My plan is that I take over the company in three years.

II. 1. An elderly gentleman came to ask me how he could get to the public library.
2. What he needs to do is contacting his assistant right away.
3. The boss has told me the reason why he fired me but I think it ridiculous.

4. I have a plan that I am going to take the kids to the amusement park tomorrow morning.

5. It is very important that you should let the others know people can trust you.

III. 1. 他出不出席会议没多大关系。

2. 据报道,迄今为止,外国金融机构已打入中国 19 个城市。

3. 书籍最大的好处不一定总是来自我们所记忆的内容,而是在于书的启迪。

4. 我们需要大家清楚,一旦你离开就再也不能回来。

5. 一些年轻的女性认为很难接受一种说法,即权利的特征经常不能在女性身上显现出来。

Unit 4　定语从句 (Adjective Clauses)

I. 1. I am talking with a woman who is curious about everything.

2. I have some good friends that are ready to offer help anytime.

3. I want to find a job that can support my family.

4. Camel is a kind of animal which you can rely on in the desert.

5. The girl managed to be enrolled by a famous university, which made her parents very proud.

II. 1. 横在街上的树枝对骑摩托车的人非常危险。

2. 切成块来卖的比萨饼在全世界各个城镇都是非常受欢迎的午餐。

3. 看电影时坐在我前面的那位女士带着一个大阔沿帽。

4. 我借钱的那个银行,贷款利息很高

5. 人们常说,电视可以让人掌握时事,紧跟科学与政治的最新发展,并且可以提供很多既有教育意义又有娱乐功能的节目。

6. A storekeeper is a person who owns or operates store.

7. As is often the case, the boss threw his bag and coat on the desk of the secretary as he came into the office.

8. He lost the paper, which made what we had done nothing.

V. 1. Many of the problems that exist today have existed since the beginning of recorded history.

2. I want to introduce you to that man who is standing over there.

3. Monkeys will eat almost anything that they can find.

4. The magazine that I read at the doctor's office had an interesting article which you ought to read.

5. It is important for all children to have at least one adult with whom they can form a loving, trusting relationship.

Unit 5　状语从句 (Adverbial Clauses)

II. 1. The man can not come because he doesn't want to be involved in this matter.

2. Strong as he is, he would feel exhausted after a whole day's work. / Although he is very strong, he would feel exhausted after a whole day's work

3. Pass me the dictionary when Jack has used it.

4. The concert is a confusion, and the band doesn't play as it used to.

5. You can borrow my mobile phone provided / if you return it to me tonight.
6. Scarcely did the thief get off the bus when he was caught by the police.
   No sooner did the thief get off the bus than he was caught by the police.
   The thief was caught by the police as soon as he got off the bus.
7. The speech was so boring that everyone felt bored.
8. He refused to tell us whether he would undertake the job.

III. 1. You haven't heard from me for such a long time because I have been really busy.
因为我最近一直很忙，所以这么久你没有收到我的信。
2. When I wrote to you six months ago—last April, I think—I was going to the university full-time and studying anthropology.
我记得六个月之前，也就是去年四月份给你写信时我正要去读大学学习人类学。
3. I have met some pretty weird people since I started this job.
自从我开始做这份工作，已经碰到一些很奇怪的人。
4. While he was walking around to see if they fit okay, he pulled from his pocket a little white mouse with pink eyes and asked for its opinion.
他一边四处走走看鞋子合不合适，一边从口袋里掏出一只粉眼睛的小白鼠，并且问他觉得这双鞋怎么样。
5. When the mouse twitched its nose, the man said, "We'll take them."
见到小白鼠抽了抽鼻子，这位男士说："这双鞋我买了。"

真题（从句）

I. 1—5 DCDAB　6—10 BDDBB　11—15 DCBCB　16—20 BCDAC
21—25 ADCBA　26—30 CACBB　31—35 ABDDD　36—40 DDADB
41—45 CBADC　46—49 BADD

II. 1. happier　2. more humorous　3. less　4. least　5. less　6. cleverest/most clever
7. latest　8. higher　9. more comfortable　10. earlier

Unit 6　There be 句型 ("There be" Sentence Pattern)

I. 1. is　2. would be　3. have been　4. should be / ought to be　5. is　6. stands　7. to be
8. is　9. being　10. must be/ might be

II. 1. There are not many kids under 3 in this kindergarten.
2. How many commercial fishermen are there in the United States?
3. Can there be some journalist taking cameras?
4. There exist hot arguments over this suggestion, doesn't there?
5. There used to be a lot of old women and children left in this village.

III. 1. 如果你靠举债度日，就没有必要考虑投资股票的事了。
2. 如果别人掌握了你的个人信息，就无法控制会发生什么事。
3. 毋庸置疑，专业和短期培训课程在我国已经越发受到人们的欢迎。
4. 难道没有一封来自老朋友的信吗？
5. 在迄今还没有产品来满足需求的领域，其机遇是很多的。

6. There was a man who had a little son that he loved very much.
7. There are no direct conflicts of interest between China and Europe.
8. There's the bell; someone is at the door.
9. There still exist many doubts in terms of this problem.
10. There is no use talking with this old stubborn.

Unit 7 强调句

1. B 2. C 3. A 4. C 5. B 6. D 7. D 8. D 9. D 10. D 11. D 12. B 13. A
14. C 15. A 16. B 17. A 18. B

Unit 8 词类和句子成分 (Parts of Speech and Members of Sentences)

I. dependence, explanation, formation, conclusion, information, movement, meaning, government, graduation, similarity, confusion, payment, agreement, advertisement, announcement, addition, decision, use, attraction, mixture

II. scientific, successful, responsible, colorful, national, revolutional, additional, helpful, personal, various, educational, meaningful, acceptable, useful, wooden, active

III. disagree, impractical, independent, uncover, incomplete, disorder, unhappy, informal, impossible, inactive, uncertain, discharge, dishonest, impolite

Unit 9 名词的数和主谓一致 (Number system of nouns and Subject-Verb Concord)

I. 1. A 2. B 3. D 4. C 5. D 6. A 7. D 8. B 9. B 10. C 11. A 12. B 13. C

II. 1. has 2. are 3. is 4. are 5. is 6. is 7. are 8. is 9. has 10. have 11. are
12. speak 13. races 14. approve 15. says 16. are 17. are 18. is 19. are
20. is/are 21. are 22. are 23. is 24. are 15. has

Unit 10 动词的种类

II. 1. kept 2. grew 3. looks 4. seemed 5. tastes 6. became 7. turned 8. is getting

III. 1. B 2. A 3. B 4. A 5. A 6. B

Unit 11 动词的时态

II. 1. C 2. D 3. A 4. A 5. D 6. B 7. C 8. B 9. C 10. D

III 1. drives 2. called, were not, was working 3. have had, am thinking
4. called, was just thinking 5. will study 6. has become, took, was, have changed
7. have not traveled, will have visited 8. are doing, talking, will be lying
9. turned, heard, had not heard, brought 10. have been thinking, have become

Unit 12 动词的语态 (Voice)

II. 1. C 2. A 3. B 4. D 5. C 6. A 7. C 8. D 9. A 10. A 11. B 12. C 13. D
14. B 15. B

III. 1. We were sent a letter the day before yesterday.

or: A letter was sent to us the day before yesterday.
2. My little brother has not washed the dishes.
3. Will he be invited to the party?
4. The highway has been closed because of the snow.
5. The earthquake destroyed lots of houses.
6. German is spoken in Austria.
7. The report must be completed by next Friday.
8. Credit cards will not be accepted.
9. We have not been brought the coffee.
   or: The coffee has not been brought to us.
10. The patient is being looked after by the nurse.

Unit 13 虚拟语气 (Subjunctive Mood)

II. 1. A 2. C 3. D 4. B 5. D 6. C 7. B 8. C 9. A 10. D 11. D 12. B 13. B 14. D 15. D

III. 1. (should) tell 2. (should) buy 3. were 4. (should) be turned down 5. hadn't eaten 6. (should) call 7. were 8. should ask 9. (should) report 10. (should) be

真题 (时态、语态及虚拟语气)

I. 1—5 CADAC 6—10 DCBCB 11—15 BBBCA 16—20 DDBDD 21—25 CCACC 26—31 DCDBDA

II. 1. had known 2. would have saved 3. would have been 4. had taken 5. (should) be
6. had fastened 7. would have avoided 8. said 9. (should) come 10. (should) refer
11. would have failed 12. (should) call 13. (should) limit 14. had not drunk
15. (should) give 16. were 17. is taken 18. was cheating 19. will have found
20. knew 21. will have produced 22. was elected 23. are not allowed
24. had been produced 25. are asked 26. will find 27. would be built 28. had joined
29. will have taken 30. be discovered 31. have gone 32. had been waiting/had waited
33. would try 34. shook 35. go 36. began 37. be done 38. were employed
39. got 40. have spent 41. has collected 42. was bought 43. had not locked
44. was playing 45. be heard 46. cooling/to be cooled 47. be kept
48. will finish/will have finished

Unit 14 分词 (Participles)

II. 1. missing 2. discussed 3. Not paying 4. wounded 5. shaking 6. stolen 7. Given
8. Having done

III. 1. This is the magazine sent to me by mail
2. The boy studying very hard is going to Harvard this fall.
3. There are several points which are indicated in his speech.
4. I want to meet the person who is working on the case.

5. Taking a walk in the street, he saw an accident.

6. Being yound, she knows quite a lot.

7. The new machine has a lot of advantages if it is compared with the old types.

8. When ice is heated, it will turn into water.

Unit 15 不定式 (Infinitives)

II. 1. A 2. A 3. B 4.B 5.A 6.C 7.D 8. B 9. D 10. A 11.C 12. D 13. C 14.D 15. C

III. 1. There are still a lot of problems for us to solve.

2. They signed an agreement to increase cooperation between their companies.

3. I'm sorry to tell you the bad news.

4. She was pleased to find her son doing so well at school.

5. I'm worrying about what to say.

6. When to meet them has not been decided.

7. We don't know where to go.

8. They are too tired to continue.

9. I expect you to come here on time.

10. They insisted to be rewarded for their efforts.

Unit 16 动名词 (gerunds)

II. 1. to make 2. going 3. going 4. working 5. buying 6. complaining, being, to create 7. to buy 8. being accept 9. being solved 10. using

III. 1. They are afraid of losing the match.

2. She doesn't mind working the night shift.

3. Taking the examination is the only way to get into the school.

4. Brushing teeth twice a day is what all dentists recommend.

5. We are looking forward to going out at the weekend.

6. Learning foreign culture helped us to communicate with foreigners.

7. His hobby is collecting stamps.

8. I really appreciate having the opportunity to take part in the project.

9. The course requires participating in six months of field studies.

真题（分词、不定式和动名词）

I. 1—5 BDAAB 6—10 ACAAD 11—15 DBACA 16—20 DBCDD 21—25 CAACD 26—30 DACCD 31—35 BBCDA 36—37 DC

II. 1. invited 2. exciting 3. coming 4. Impressed 5. interested 6. completed 7. playing 8. Being watched 9. Taking 10. asked 11. suggested 12. Given 13. decorated 14. Judging 15. taken 16. written 17. sitting 18. crossing 19. drawing 20. standing 21. heard 22. knocked 23. to visit 24. to get 25. searching 26. to type 27. to attend 28. not to speak 29. to put 30. to rise 31. to live 32. to take 33. to spend

34. to learn   35. not to know   36. to say   37. launching   38. learning   39. stealing
40. bargaining   41. waiting   42. working   43. spelling   44. helping   45. learning
46. to lock   47. driving   48. getting   49. having   50. joking   51. seeing   52. eating

Unit 17 冠词 (Articles)

1. A   2. A   3. A   4. D   5. B   6. B   7. D   8. C   9. A   10. C   11. D   12. A   13. B
14. B   15. D   16. A   17. D   18. A   19. D   20. A

Unit 18 介词 (Prepositions)

I. 1. of   2. to   3. from   4. from   5. for   6. in   7. with   8. of   9. from   10. with   11. at
12. for   13. in   14. by   15. with   16. By, for   17. with   18. to, by   19. to, at
20. in, from

II. 1. A   2. A   3. B   4. D   5. A   6. C   7. D   8. B   9. A   10. D   11. B   12. C   13. B
14. B   15. C   16. A   17. B   18. A   19. B   20. B

Unit 19 形容词和副词

1. C   2. A   3. A   4. B   5. C   6. C   7. B   8. A   9. A   10. C   11. D   12. B   13. D
14. C   15. B   16. A   17. A   18. C   19. C   20. B

Unit 20 形容词和副词的比较级和最高级

1. B   2. B   3. B   4. B   5. C   6. A   7. D   8. D   9. A   10. C   11. A   12. B   13. C
14. D   15. A   16. D   17. C   18. A   19. A

Unit 21 不定代词 (Indefinite Pronouns)

1. C   2. A   3. A   4. D   5. C   6. A   7. B   8. A   9. C   10. B   11. B   12. D   13. D

真题 (其他类型)

I. 1—5 BDACC   6—10 BCDDD   11—15 ABACC   16—20 CBBAB   21-25 BDBDC
    26—30 BCDCA   31—34 BDCC

II. 1. walk   2. were told   3. was questioned   4. is   5. knows   6. are   7. musician
    8. hard-working   9. practical   10. misunderstanding   11. entirely   12. difference
    13. employee   14. performance   15. extremely   16. fasten   17. appointment
    18. settlement   19. widen   20. economic   21. additional   22. reasonable   23. proposal
    24. eagerly   25. strength   26. equipment   27. successful   28. qualified
    29. internationally   30. receptionist   31. objection   32. response   33. costly   34. golden
    35. protection   36. permission   37. heavily   38. musical   39. fortunately
    40. withdrawals   41. protection   42. modernize   43. arrival   44. healthy/healthful
    45. consideration   46. extremely   47. desirable   48. dangerous   49. operation
    50. attractive   51. friendly   52. exciting   53. certainly   54. development   55. helpful
    56. excited   57. expensive   58. shorten   59. effective   60. foreigner   61. achievement

62. confident 63. invitation 64. really 65. disappointed 66. lucky 67. illness
68. successful 69. painting 70. highly 71. waiting 72. operation 73. certainly
74. management 75. confidence 76. really 77. practical 78. application
79. reasonable 80. difference 81. unnecessarily 82. employees 83. monthly
84. apparently 85. loudly 86. growth 87. shorten

参考文献 (References)

1. Azar, Betty Schrampfer(美),《朗文中级英语语法》,西安交通大学出版社,2008。
2. Molinsky, Steven J. & Bill Bliss,《朗文国际英语教程》(1—4册),上海外语教育出版社,2007。
3. 薄冰:《高级英语语法》,高等教育出版社,1999。
4. 薄冰:《通用英语语法》,商务印书馆国际有限公司,2009。
5. 常红梅:《北京地区成人本科学士学位英语统一考试辅导》,中国人民大学出版社,2007。
6. 戴立黎:《高等学校英语应用能力考试A级历年全真试卷与译文详解》,中央民族大学出版社,2006。
7. 戴立黎:《高等学校英语应用能力考试B级历年全真试卷与译文详解》,中央民族大学出版社,2006。
8. 高远:《大学英语自学教程》(上册、下册),高等教育出版社,2005。
9. 龚耀:《高等学校英语应用能力考试精讲精练》,外语教学与研究出版社,2007。
10. 郭梅、王进思:《高职高专"专升本"英语应用能力考试A级专项训练综合指导》,北京大学出版社,2006。
11. 黄建滨:《新世纪英语教程 专科·语法》,浙江大学出版社,2005。
12. 李基安:《现代英语语法》,外语教学与研究出版社,2000。
13. 李银芳、赵冬生:《大学英语简明语法》,黑龙江人民出版社,2006。
14. 林健、安维彧:《英语应用能力考试分项训练(B)》,天津大学出版社,2007。
15. 全国高等学校英语教学命题研究组:《全国高等学校英语应用能力考试全真模拟试题及详解B级》,学林出版社,2004。
16. 王振芳:《新编实用英语语法》,高等教育出版社,2005。
17. 吴祯福:《英语高级口语》,外语教学与研究出版社,2008。
18. 吴祯福:《英语中级口语》,外语教学与研究出版社,2007。
19. 徐广联:《大学英语语法讲座与测试》,华东理工大学出版社,2001。
20. 闫文培:《高等学校英语应用能力考试A级演练与测试题集》,外语教学与研究出版社,2004。
21. 闫文培:《高等学校英语应用能力考试B级演练与测试题集》,外语教学与研究出版社,2004。
22. 张道真:《实用英语语法》,外语教学与研究出版社,1995。
23. 张克礼:《新英语语法》,高等教育出版社,2001。
24. 章振邦:《新编英语语法教程》,上海外语教育出版社,2004。
25. 赵立民:《商务英语听说手册》,对外经济贸易大学出版社,2007。
26. 郑仰成、李育、毛洁:《简明实用英语语法》,高等教育出版社,2008。

21世纪商务英语系列教材

本套教材兼有英语语言能力与国际商务专业知识双重教学任务。在教材安排上给学生充足的语言材料和联系情景,同时以清晰的专业理论讲解为基础,使学生在掌握了理论知识的基础上,学习词汇和句型,力求达到学以致用的目的。

采用英语编写,英语和专业知识融合一体:给学习者提供了大量的外贸语言素材,能帮助学习者更好地理解各章的专业和英语知识;形式多样的练习可以有效地帮助学习者提高实际运用能力。

结构合理,体系完整新颖:该套教材强调核心技能培养的渗透性,按照教学流程设计编写体例,循序渐进地、潜移默化地培养学生的专业核心技能和语言实际运用能力。教学活动设计充分体现讲练结合原则、任务教学原则、师生互动原则、实践性原则。

国际商务英语概要	29.50	张九明
商务英语阅读教程	29.80	王元歌
国际贸易实务	30.00	丁静辉
商务英语信函写作	32.00	王元歌
商务英语应用文写作与翻译	26.00	林　静
实用商务英语写作	42.00	蒋　磊
国际商务英语函电	28.50	蒋　磊
商务英语听说(上)	25.00(配有光盘)	潘月洲
商务英语听说(下)	28.00(配有光盘)	潘月洲
商务英语阅读(上)	25.00	扬　远
商务英语阅读(下)	25.00	陆松岩

北京大学出版社

外语编辑部电话:010-62767347　　　市场营销部电话:010-62750672
　　　　　　　010-62755217　　　邮购部电话:010-62752015
　　　Email: zbing@pup.pku.edu.cn

英语写作原版影印系列丛书

本丛书为北京大学出版社最新引进的一套国外英语写作畅销书。本套教材邀请了部分国内专家撰写中文导读,对教材的作者、特色、使用对象和方法介绍,就各章节主要内容进行简述。

本套丛书是我国引进国外优秀的英语写作教学与研究成果,对更新我国的英语写作教学观念和方法,改革当前的英语写作教学具有十分重要的意义。

本套丛书可供全国大专院校的学生、社会读者和写作爱好者学习英语写作使用,也可以作为英语写作教师开设写作课的教材和参考书。

—— 王立非

公司管理写作策略	Steven H. Gale Mark Garrison
数字时代写作研究策略(第2版)	Bonnie L. Tensen
分析性写作(第5版)	David Rosenwasser Jill Stephen
实用写作(第9版)	Edward P. Bailey Philip A. Powell
成功写作入门(第10版)	Jean Wyrick
跨课程论文写作(第5版)	Susan M. Hubbuch
毕业论文及研究论文写作	P. Paul Heppner Mary J. Heppner
学术论文写作手册(第7版)	Anthony C. Winkler Jo Ray McCuen-Metherell

北京大学 出版社
外语编辑部电话:010-62767347　　市场营销部电话:010-62750672
　　　　　　　010-62755217　　邮 购 部 电话:010-62752015
Email: zbing@pup.pku.edu.cn